NOTABLE SOUTHERN FAMILIES

VOLUME VI

COMPILED BY
ZELLA ARMSTRONG

JANAWAY PUBLISHING, INC.
Santa Maria, California

Notice

In many older books, foxing (or discoloration) occurs and, in some instances, print lightens with wear and age. Reprinted books, such as this, often duplicate these flaws, notwithstanding efforts to reduce or eliminate them. The pages of this reprint have been digitally enhanced and, where possible, the flaws eliminated in order to provide clarity of content and a pleasant reading experience.

Notable Southern Families. Volume VI

Copyright © 1933, by Zella Armstrong

Originally published
Chattanooga, Tennessee
1933

Reprinted by:

Janaway Publishing, Inc.
732 Kelsey Ct.
Santa Maria, California 93454
(805) 925-1038
www.janawaygenealogy.com

2017

ISBN: 978-1-59641-389-4

Made in the United States of America

Reverend Samuel Doak, D.D.

This book is lovingly dedicated
to the memory of
all Tennessee preachers,
and especially to my husband,
REV. JOHN STEWART FRENCH,
and his father,
REV. JOHN LEE MCCARTY FRENCH,
also his grandfather,
REV. GEORGE STEWART.

PREFACE

In writing the history of the Doak Family of Tennessee, the author has attempted to uphold the prestige of the *Notable Southern Families* series in compiling and preserving for future generations the history and genealogy of some remarkable pioneers in the State of Tennessee.

Reverend Samuel Doak, D.D., was a "triple pioneer" if one may use that term in connection with so distinguished a person.

First—he was a pioneer in the typical sense, from the Mother state of Virginia to that of her fair daughter, Tennessee.

Second—he was a pioneer preacher—Presbyterian—and was doubtless the first of that denomination, or any denomination, to *reside* in the Tennessee country.

Third—he was a pioneer educator—the founder of the first institution of learning (Washington College), in the Tennessee country. In this connection he organized the first library, not only in Tennessee, but the first west of the Alleghenies.

Tennessee and the whole Southwest owe much to this great man whose two splendid sons—Rev. John Whitfield Doak, and Rev. Samuel Witherspoon Doak—followed in his footsteps as preachers and teachers.

In presenting this book we feel that we are preserving for posterity a valuable part of the history of Tennessee, namely, the religious and educational life, the seed of which was sown by men like Reverend Charles Cummings, Reverend Samuel Houston, and Reverend Samuel Doak.

We do not claim that we have compiled a complete genealogy of the descendants of Samuel Doak. It has been impossible to locate descendants of some of his children. Many members of the family, however, have aided in the preparation of this account and we wish to acknowledge with grateful thanks our indebtedness to the following relatives and friends, and many others:

Mr. and Mrs. Charles E. Colle, Greeneville, Tenn.; Mr. and Mrs. Thomas Ross Preston, Chattanooga, Tenn.; Reverend A. Sidney Doak, Huntsville, Alabama; Mr. Charles S. Doak, Tusculum, Tennessee; Miss Mary Burt Rankin, Buffalo, New York; Mr. Charles Doak Lowry, Chicago, Illinois; Miss Hannah Doak, Johnson City, Tennessee; Miss Bessie Collup, Johnson City, Tenn.; Mrs. Joseph Warren Keifer, Jr., Bostwick, Nebraska; Mrs. John T. Moore, Bartlesville, Oklahoma; Mrs. Allan Shaw,

Bartlesville, Oklahoma; Mrs. Lucy Lowry Conn, Superior, Nebraska; Mrs. Harris Crawford, Pittsburgh, Pennsylvania; Judge Samuel Doak Catherwood, Austin, Minnesota; Mrs. E. Lockert Doak, Nashville, Tennessee; Mrs. Archibald Alexander Doak, Nashville, Tennessee; Mr. and Mrs. Eugene Coile, Nashville, Tennessee; and to Mr. Thomas W. Preston, President of the King Printing Company, Bristol, Tenn.

JANIE C. FRENCH.

Birmingham, Alabama,

July, 1933.

TABLE OF CONTENTS

CHAPTER   I—GENEALOGY OF THE EMIGRANT DOAKS.

CHAPTER   II—GENEALOGY OF THE REVEREND SAMUEL DOAK, D.D.

CHAPTER   III—OTHER DOAK LINES.

CHAPTER   IV—SKETCH OF REVEREND SAMUEL DOAK, D.D.

CHAPTER   V—WASHINGTON COLLEGE.

CHAPTER   VI—MISCELLANEOUS RECORDS.

CHAPTER   VII—DOAK WILLS.

CHAPTER VIII—MATHEWS-MATHES.

CHAPTER I
GENEALOGY OF THE EMIGRANT DOAKS

"Happy he who remembers his progenitors with pride, who relates with pleasure to the listener the story of their greatness, of their deeds and silently rejoicing sees himself linked to the end of this goodly chain."
GOETHE.

(Plan of this book for the generations is as follows: Roman numerals, equal the names of *children* of Rev. Samuel Doak; open numerals equal his *grandchildren;* numerals in brackets equal his *great-grandchildren;* letters in brackets equal his *great-great-grandchildren,* etc.)

SAMUEL DOAK, first of the family whom we know, lived and died in County Antrim of the Province of Ulster, Ireland, where we find the name spelled Doach, Doage, Doack, Doak, etc.

His sons, John, Nathaniel, Robert, David, and Samuel Doak, with their sister, Thankful, and probably another sister, Julia, emigrated to America about 1740, settling for a short time in East Nottingham Township, Chester county, Pennsylvania, and moving thence to Augusta county, Virginia, where on September 23, 1741, a deed was granted to the emigrant, Samuel Doak, by William Beverley, owner of the Beverly Manor Estates.

Samuel Doak was a member of company 4, Va., Augusta Co., Rangers in 1742. (Croziers' Va. Col. Militia, p. 92).

While it is the purpose of this book to follow the line of the Emigrant Samuel, father of the Reverend Samuel Doak, D.D., of Tennessee, notes regarding the other emigrants of his father's family will be given first.

EMIGRANT NATHANIEL DOAK

We have no records of Nathaniel's brother, Emigrant John Doak, other than several mentions to be found in the Augusta county records—one of which we quote: "John Doak (Doache) a member of Capt. John Christian's Co." (Chalkleys' Vol. II, p. 509).

Rev. B. E. Hanes, of Elkins, West Virginia, has written a book about still another Doak family which emigrated to America in 1800. In this book Rev. Hanes quotes several letters, among them one from Rev. D. B. Doak of Plain View, Texas, a descendant of the Emigrant Nathaniel Doak, which says in part: "My great-grandfather, Nathaniel Doak, had the following children: John, Alexander Shields, Thomas, Sophia, Margaret Elizabeth, Ann Eliza, and Lavania. These moved about a hundred years ago to Missouri. Alexander Shields Doak, my grandfather, had four children: Jane, Peter Porter, Alexander Shields, jr., and Henry Bascom Doak. The latter was my father. I have two brothers, William and Charles. Others of the name in Texas are: Hugh, Charles and Doctor Doak.

"My great-grandfather's brother, Robert (the emigrant), later rose to Colonel and was for some time in the Virginia Legislature."

EMIGRANT ROBERT DOAK

We find in the Chalkley's records of Augusta county, Virginia, the following: "Robert Doak, the emigrant, married ——— Breckenridge, a sister of Robert Breckenridge." Also: "James Doak, son of Robert, the emigrant, and ——— Breckenridge, married Jane Dunn."

This latter record corroborates a letter in the Doak Book by Rev. B. E. Hanes, which states: "This son, James, born 1760, had a son, Joseph, born 1786, who had a son named Robert, born 1815, whose daughter was my mother." This letter was signed by N. B. Mavity, French Lick, Indiana.

According to Mrs. Margaret Logan Morris, of Corydon, Indiana (who has written a history of "The Irvins, Doaks, Logans, and McCampbells of Kentucky and Virginia of Virginia"), this Emigrant Robert Doak lived near the town of Mount Crawford, in Rockingham county, Virginia.

In 1753 a party of Rangers passed through the vicinity of Mount Crawford and spoke of Robert Doak's beautiful plantation, good water, etc. Of the children of Robert Doak, Mrs. Morris quotes the following:

1. James, b. 1760, in Rockbridge county, Virginia.

2. Robert, married —— Breckenridge. He went to Kentucky. His name is on the Fayette county court records as early as 1776.

3. Joseph W. Doak.

4. Mary Doak, married —— Breckenridge.

5. Jane Doak, married James Dunn, son of James and Martha Long Dunn. His will was proven June 29, 1849.

EMIGRANT DAVID DOAK

The will of Emigrant David Doak was probated October 2, 1787, in Montgomery county, Virginia, and mentions: "Wife, Mary; sons, David, Samuel, Nathaniel, William, James, Robert, Thomas, Alexander and John; daus., Elizabeth, Jane, Mary and Margaret."

William N. Doak, former Secretary of Labor, of Washington, D. C., is a descendant of the Emigrant David's son, John Doak, born 1762, married Rebecca Wilson in 1805, and had Audley (Edley) Doak (b. 1807, d. 1897), who married Elizabeth Creger (b. 1821, d. 1893). Their son, Reverend Canaro Dragtun Doak (b. 1843, d. 1919), married in 1865 Elizabeth Dutton (b. 1844, d. 1931), and were the parents of the above William N. Doak, the late Mrs. Lula Doak McCarty (Mrs. D. F.), of Bristol, Va., who died April 19,

1933, and Mr. Edward Doak, of Detroit, Michigan, who died February, 1933, also Mrs. Myra Doak Seagle, deceased.

The old home of William N. Doak is a part of the original tract known as the Black Lick (sometimes called "Black Buffalo Lick"), comprising a part of what is now Wythe county, near Rural Retreat, Virginia. Deeds of hundreds of acres of this plot to the Emigrant David and Mary Doak were made as early as 1748, and since then the immediate family of former Secretary Doak has owned the land.

EMIGRANT DOAK SISTERS

The consensus of opinion, based upon family and historical records, prove that at least TWO (probably three) Doak sisters emigrated from Ireland with their brothers in 1740, namely, Ann and Thankful—some say, also, Julia.

Ann Doak married George Breckenridge (see data under "Breckenridge" in back of this book).

Thankful Doak married John Finley of Princeton, N. J., and they were the parents of Samuel Finley, former president of what was then Princeton College, New Jersey.

The Emigrant Samuel Doak (brother of Thankful) mentions in his will "Brother-in-law John Finley."

The Colonial records of Pennsylvania Archives, Vol. I, p. 436, dated March 16, 1749, mention among other Justices of Cumberland county, the name of John Finley.

For further records of John Finley, who married Thankful Doak, see p. 369, Vol. V, *Notable Southern Families*—CROCKETT FAMILY—by French and Armstrong, which gives the line from the Emigrant James Finley (father of John), down to that of Polly (Mary) Finley, who married Tennessee's illustrious son, Colonel David ("Davy") Crockett, hero of the Alamo, whose ancestral line is traced out to the Court of Louis the XIV; while the wife of his youth—Polly Finley—goes one better and has her line traced back to the house of Macbeth, in 1009.

EMIGRANT SAMUEL DOAK

We find in Chaulkley's records of Augusta county, Virginia, that the Emigrant Samuel Doak married on the voyage to America Jane Mitchell. He does not state that she was a widow, though there is a clause in the will of the Emigrant Samuel which suggests the possibility that Jane Mitchell had been previously married. The clause reads: "To wife, Jane, and *her* three daughters, Elinor, Mary and Isel."

The emigrants, Samuel and Jane Mitchell Doak, settled first in Chester county, Pennsylvania, for a short time before removing to Augusta county, Virginia, where they made their home. Among the Augusta county records is to be found a deed to the said Emigrant Samuel Doak, by William Beverley, of Beverley Manor, dated September 23, 1741.

Samuel Doak and his brother, John Doak, were in Captain John Christian's Company—1742. (See Chaulkley, Vol. II, pp. 32 and 509). Samuel Doak was also a Constable in 1755 —and a surveyor in Captain James Mitchell's company. For further military and other records of the Doak family, see in the back of this book.

The will of Emigrant Samuel Doak was proven May 19, 1772, in Augusta county, Virginia, and mentions besides— "Wife, Jane, and her three daughters," sons: David, John, Samuel, Robert, and daughters: Jane and Elizabeth (Elizabeth Thankful).

Children of Samuel and Jane Mitchell Doak:

1. Elinor, married Judge Campbell of the Superior Court of Ohio.
2. Isel (Isabel). No records.
3. John. No records.
4. Jane, married William Brown.
5. David, eldest son, married Jennie Alexander.
6. Samuel (Rev.), born 1749; married first, Esther Houston Montgomery; married second, Mrs. Margaretta (Houston) McEwen. (See more later).

7. Robert, married first, ——— Campbell; married second, Mrs. McGuffin and had a son, Col. Samuel Alexander Doak, who married Margaret Shields, of Mount Crawford, Virginia, a granddaughter of Thankful Doak and John Finley, whose daughter married James Shields. Col. S. A. Doak, and Margaret Shields Doak, had issue: David, Polly, Ella, Fannie and Amzy Doak.

8. Mary (or Nancy), married Abner Weatherly, of Wilkes county, North Carolina.

CHILDREN:—*Weatherly*.

(1) Madison, married Mary Batey.

(2) Nancy, b. 1808—married Alexander Hamilton Coffey in Wilkes county, N. C., 1826; she died 1841. Children: (a) Rice Coffey, married his cousin, Mary Coffey; (b) Avery Coffey married Elizabeth Harris; (c) Napoleon Coffey.

(3) Frances, b. March 3, 1817; died August 8, 1854, and is buried near Murfreesboro, Tenn., in Rutherford county. She married William Henry Halliburton, and had Mary Pocahontas Halliburton, born August 14, 1840; died June 28, 1927; married December 15, 1857, in Rutherford county, Tennessee, to Warren Franklin Hooper, born October 11, 1839, had issue:

(a) Cora Hooper, born June 24, 1861; died Mar. 7, 1927; married Dr. D. L. Delk.

(b) Warnie Hooper, married Jonathan Dayton in Chattanooga, Tenn., Nov. 11, 1895; had issue:

Ruth Hooper, born Dec. 23, 1897—engaged in journalistic work, and now (1933) in southern France doing research work.

William Hooper, born Nov. 2, 1902; a

journalist—on Wall Street Journal in New York City.

Jonathan Hooper, born Feb. 12, 1900, was entirely destroyed, May 18, 1918, in Oakdale, Pennsylvania, while making gas for the United States Government.

Jonathan Dayton (who married Warnie Hooper) died June 17, 1904, at White Sulphur Springs, Alabama, and is buried in Chattanooga, Tennessee. He was a son of Amos Cooper Dayton (descended from Fenimore Cooper, the famous writer) and Lucinda Harrison.

Amos Cooper Dayton was a son of Jonathan Dayton, one of the signers of the Federal Constitution, and traces his lineage back to Ralph DAYGTON, who was born 1588 in Yorkshire, England.

Mrs. Jonathan Dayton (Warnie Hooper), married second, on March 17, 1923, to Lowndes Turney, a prominent lawyer of Chattanooga, Tennessee, who was a son of Ex-Governor Pete Turney. Mrs. Turney is prominent in club and patriotic organizations—having been State President of the Tennessee Daughters of the Confederacy.

9. Elizabeth Thankful Doak (dau. of Samuel the Emigrant) married Major William Hall (b. 1740), and they were parents of Governor William Hall of Tennessee.

Rev. Samuel Doak's first visit to Tennessee was to the Watauga settlement (now Elizabethton) to visit his sister, Mrs. Elizabeth Thankful Doak Hall, who lived near the old Hall's Ford on the Watauga River, where many of her descendants still reside.

Major William Hall (son of Richard Hall of Ireland) lived in Surry county, North Carolina, where he received his appointment in 1776 as major in the Revolutionary War. In 1779 he sold his possessions in North Carolina and removed with his family to New River, Virginia, where he lived for five years, moving thence to Sumner county, Tennessee, in 1785, where he and his wife and children suffered from Indian atrocities. He and two of his sons were killed by Indians in Sumner county, Aug. 3, 1787.

CHILDREN :—*Hall.*

(1) Mary, married first Captain John Morgan, a Revolutionary soldier; married second, William Cage.

Their eldest daughter, Nancy Morgan, married James Bright, of Kentucky, who was a surveyor and settled at Fayetteville, about 1803, where Captain Morgan also settled about the same time. James and Nancy Morgan Bright had a son, General John Morgan Bright. Mrs. J. L. Caldwell, Misses Mary, Sarah and Margaret Bright, Gardner and Morgan Bright of Chattanooga, Tennessee, and Mrs. Judith Bright Gracey, of Augusta, Ga., are descendants of this family.

(2) James Hall was killed by Indians in 1785, the first white person killed in what is now Middle Tennessee.

(3) Richard Hall was killed by Indians when his father was killed Aug. 3, 1787.

(4) Sarah Hall married, first, Andrew Lynum; second, James Anderson. Through these marriages are descended a branch of the Anderson and Whiteside families of Chattanooga, Tennessee.

(5) William Hall was Governor of Tennessee and married Mary Alexander.

(6) John Hall.

(7) Prudence Hall.

We next take up the line of Mrs. Elizabeth Thankful Doak Hall's brother, the Reverend Samuel Doak, pioneer preacher and teacher of Tennessee.

CHAPTER II
GENEALOGY OF THE REVEREND SAMUEL DOAK, D.D.

The famous Tennessee minister and educator, Samuel Doak, was often called "The Father of Education in Tennessee." He was born August 1, 1749, in Augusta county, Virginia, and died December 12, 1830, at his home in Washington county, Tennessee. (See sketch of his life).

He was married on Oct. 31, 1775, in the New Providence Church, Augusta county, Virginia, to Esther Houston Montgomery, daughter of John Montgomery, who emigrated to America about 1730 and settled in Pennsylvania, where he married about 1751, Esther Houston. They moved from Pennsylvania to Augusta county, Virginia, settling between Staunton and Lexington, near New Providence Church.

Esther Houston emigrated to America from Ireland about 1735, with her parents, John and Margaret Cunningham Houston, who remained in Pennsylvania until their three eldest children were married. (For further data on Montgomery and Houston lines—see p. 167, Vol. V, *Notable Southern Families*, CROCKETT FAMILY—by French and Armstrong; for Houston data see Vol. II, p. 179, of *Notable Southern Families*, by Armstrong).

Rev. Samuel Doak's first wife—Esther Houston Montgomery, was born 1760; died July 3, 1807, and is buried in Salem Cemetery, Washington county, Tennessee. He married second, in 1818, Mrs. Margaretta Houston McEwen, widow of Alexander McEwen, and sister of Rev. Samuel Houston; she died Sept. 22, 1831, and is buried in the New Salem Cemetery, where lies the body of the Reverend Samuel Doak. No issue by the second marriage.

The Doak Family

Children of Rev. Samuel Doak:

I. Julia Doak, born Aug. 10, 1776; married Adam Lowry. (More later).

II. John Whitfield Doak, born Oct. 18, 1778; married Jane H. Alexander. (More later).

III. Lucinda Doak, born May 23, 1782, in Washington county, Tenn.; died 1825 in Illinois; married ——— Baldridge.

IV. Samuel Witherspoon Doak, born Mar. 24, 1785; married Sarah Houston McEwen. (More later).

V. Jane Rowe Doak, born Sept. 13, 1787, in Washington county, Tennessee (then State of Franklin); died January, 1828. She is buried at Harmony Cemetery, Greeneville, Tenn.; married David Rice. We have been unable to secure the names of all their children, but one of their children was named John Holt Rice (1825-1911), married Nancy Russell (1827-1911), in 1847. John and Nancy Russell Rice had a son, William Montgomery Rice, born 1850, married Florence Stephenson, born 1861. They had among other children Ethelyn Rice, who married Ernest Hadden Haskell, and reside in Oklahoma City, Okla. Another daughter, Flora Rice, married Paul Giddings, and resides in Anoka, Minnesota.

VI. Polly (Mary) Montgomery Doak, born June 19, 1792, married a Mr. Davit. Have no further records of this line.

VII. Nancy Doak, born June 9, 1790, married first William Mitchell (1771-1827); married second Adam Broyles, in 1825—no issue by second marriage. Standing somewhat off the road between Washington College and Limestone is the old Broylesville Inn, which was opened by Adam Broyles.

CHILDREN:—*Mitchell.*

1. Samuel Mitchell, born 1812, married Amelia Fain. Children:

(1) William Mitchell; (2) Elizabeth Mitchell, married Seburn J. Galbreath; (3) Thomas Mitchell, married Eva Perry.

(2) Esther (Susannah) Montgomery Mitchell, born 1815; died 1832; married in 1838 to George J. Allen (b. 1809, d. 1850). They moved to Calhoun, Missouri, in a covered wagon. Their son, William Montgomery Allen (b. 1838, d. 1914), married in 1870 Julia Miller Harris, and their daughter, Annie Allen, married John Boyd, of Henry county, Missouri.

(3) David Mitchell—unmarried.

(4) William Montgomery Mitchell, born Feb. 13, 1823, married Rachel Ellen Anderson, daughter of Samuel Anderson, and sister of the late John Fain Anderson, who were grandchildren of Col. John Fain, of Tennessee.

CHILDREN:—*Mitchell.*

(a) Addie Doak Mitchell, unmarried, Limestone, Tenn.
(b) Samuel Fain Mitchell, unmarried; died 1927.
(c) William Hugh Mitchell, unmarried.
(d) Stella Mitchell, unmarried.

We will now take up in detail the lines of three of Rev. Samuel Doak's children, namely: Julia Doak, who married Adam Lowry, and Rev. John Whitfield Doak, also Rev. Samuel Witherspoon Doak.

1. JULIA DOAK LOWRY

Julia Doak (dau. of Rev. Samuel), was born in Augusta county, Virginia, August 10, 1776; married Adam Lowry in Washington county, Tennessee, 1794.

Adam Lowry came from County Derry, Ireland, about

1765, and died 1826. Julia Doak Lowry died 1857. Both she and her husband are buried in Ripley, Ohio, where they died.

CHILDREN:—*Lowry.*

1. Jean G. Lowry, b. Dec. 1, 1795; m. Rev. John Rankin —more later.
2. Esther Montgomery Lowry, b. Jan. 22, 1798; m. Patric Carey—more.
3. Samuel Gardner Lowry, b. Mar. 26, 1800; see more later.
4. Eliza Rowe Lowry, b. Jan. 10, 1808; m. Rev. Robt. H. Rankin—more later.
5. Mary Merriwether Lowry, b. June 6, 1810; m. Rev. A. T. Rankin—more.
6. William Ramsey Lowry, b. Sept. 20, 1816; see more later.
7. Lucinda Lowry, b. about 1818; m. William McNish —more later.
8. Julia Rowe Lowry, the records regarding this daughter have been rather conflicting and so far no one of the descendants can correct the error. One record states she married Rev. Alexander Rankin! another states she married James McConaughy, of Ripley, Ohio, who died in less than a year after their marriage, and that she died three weeks later—hence no correct records seem available.
9. John Knox Lowry—of whom we have no records.

We now take up the records of the first seven children in detail.

1. JEAN GILFILLEN LOWRY was born Dec. 1, 1795; married in Washington county, Tennessee, to Rev. John Rankin, Jan. 2, 1816. She died in Ripley, Ohio, Dec. 28, 1878. They had thirteen children and six of their sons were in the War Between the States.

CHILDREN:—*Rankin.*

(1) Rev. Adam Lowry, born Nov. 4, 1816, was Captain of the 13th Illinois Regiment.

GENEALOGY OF THE REVEREND SAMUEL DOAK, D.D. 21

- (2) Isabella Jane, born June 16, 1818.
- (3) David, born Sept. 18, 1819.
- (4) Richard Calvin, born July 24, 1821, was Captain of the 7th Ohio Volunteer Company.
- (5) Rev. Samuel G. W., born Dec. 28, 1822, was in the 11th Corps under Hooker.
- (6) Julia Doak, born Nov. 2, 1824.
- (7) John Thompson, born Feb. 25, 1826, was with the 116th Illinois.
- (8) Dr. Andrew Campbell, born June 22, 1828, was assistant surgeon in 88th Illinois.
- (9) Mary Eliza, born Feb. 21, 1830.
- (10) William Alexander, born Sept. 15, 1831—see more later.
- (11) Lucinda, born May 3, 1834.
- (12) Arthur T., born Mar. 5, 1836.
- (13) Thomas L., born Jan. 16, 1839.

(10) WILLIAM ALEXANDER RANKIN (son of Rev. John) was born in Ripley, Ohio, Sept. 15, 1831, and died in Albuquerque, New Mexico, Jan. 11, 1897. He was Captain and Assistant Quartermaster of the 1st Division, C.C.-M.D.M. He was married in Columbus, Ohio, Jan. 2, 1852, to Phoebe D. Ward (b. Jan. 9, 1832), daughter of Fordham Ward and Rebecca Meeks, who was a daughter of Elijah Meeks and Lucy Williams Meeks.

CHILDREN:—*Rankin.*

- (a) Amanda Julia, b. Dec. 29, 1852, in Columbus, Ohio; died Aug. 10, 1929—unmarried.
- (b) Frank Oswin, b. Jan., 1854; died in infancy.
- (c) Lou Rankin, born Sept. 20, 1856, in Paris, Illinois; married Oct. 6, 1885, in Lawrence, Kansas, to John T. Moore, a son of George and Elizabeth Moore of

London, England. John T. Moore was born in London, England, May 1, 1855.

Children: Oreta Elizabeth Moore was born Sept. 2, 1889, at Lawrence, Kansas; married June 4, 1917, Allan Reese Shaw (b. Sept. 6, 1888, in Lima, Ohio), a son of Thomas Reese Shaw and Fanny Haliday Shaw.

Children of Oreta and Allan Shaw: Robert Rankin Shaw, b. Dec. 11, 1928—adopted—son of Alice Rankin and Gordon Brent. This baby was adopted by Mr. and Mrs. Allan Shaw upon the death of the child's mother. The second son of Mr. and Mrs. Allan Shaw is John Reese Shaw, born Dec. 6, 1930.

(d) Don J. Rankin, born Oct. 26, 1858, at Black Jack, Kansas; married Alice Collier, who was born in Pittsburgh, Pa., June 21, 1860.

Children: (1) Herbert W. Rankin, b. Sept. 25, 1885, at Lawrence, Kansas; married Alice Templin (b. Sept. 23, 1887), daughter of Olin Templin and Lena Van Voorhis; children—Alice Herberta Rankin, b. Sept. 24, 1909; married Gordon Brent; their son, Robert, was born Dec. 11, 1928—the mother died and the baby Robert was adopted by his aunt, Mrs. Allan Shaw, and Mr. Shaw. Mary Jane Rankin, b. Jan. 28, 1913. Helen Barbara Rankin, b. May 12, 1920. (2) Madonna Alice Rankin, b. May 6, 1887, at Lawrence, Kansas; married at Albuquerque, New Mexico, Sept. 6, 1911, to Albert P. Learned (b. June 14, 1888), a son of S. Stanley Learned and Alice Preisach Learned; children: Alice Rankin

Learned, b. Oct. 5, 1912, at Kansas City, Mo.; Ruth Eleanor Learned, b. Aug. 1, 1916, at Kansas City, Mo.; Margaret Louise Learned, b. Nov. 11, 1919. (3) Juanita Gertrude Rankin, b. July 12, 1889, in New Mexico; married Howard Ashley Parker, Oct. 8, 1912, at New Mexico. Children: Howard Ashley Parker, Jr., b. Dec. 26, 1922, at Tulsa, Okla.; they have a son, Donald Edwin, b. Dec. 15, 1925. (4) Zella Marguerite Rankin, b. Sept. 19, 1897, New Mexico, married Edmund Phillip Learned (of Lawrence, Kansas), at Albuquerque, New Mexico, Aug. 30, 1922, a son of Stanley and Alice Learned. Children of Zella and Edmund Learned: Betty Lucile, b. Jan. 27, 1924, and Don Rankin Learned, b. July 25, 1925, at Kansas City, Mo.

(e) Harry Rankin (son of Wm. A.), born Jan. 3, 1863, in Lawrence, Kansas, and died in New York; married first, Oct. 8, 1884, Ora Good, of Lawrence, Kansas; she was born August, 1865, and died at Ashville, Ky., in 1905. He married second, Ella Jameson—they have one son, Talby Rankin, b. 1910. Children by first wife: (1) Roger Rankin, b. Aug. 4, 1885; married Ellen Rule, of Kansas City, Mo.—they have Wm. Roger, b. Nov. 13, 1916, and Charles Rule, b. Dec. 22, 1922. (2) Earl Rankin, b. Sept. 9, 1887; married in Kansas City, and lives in New York City. (3) George Rankin, b. Aug. 24, 1889; died Dec. 20, 1927; was Captain in the Army and is buried at Arlington Cemetery; he left one daughter,

Gloria, who was born at Albuquerque, New Mexico.

(f) Fred William Rankin (son of Wm. A.), born Apr. 29, 1869, at Lawrence, Kansas; died Aug., 1911, at Kansas City, Mo.; married Jessie Darr of Chicago, Illinois. Children: (1) Jean A. Rankin, b. Oct. 30, 1897; married Frank Siegfield of Higginsville, Mo.; children —Frances Louise, b. Feb. 17, 1920; Teresa Lucile, b. Aug. 8, 1922; Charles Leslie, b. Oct. 15, 1929. (2) Helen Rankin, b. Sept. 18, 1900. (3) Marian Rankin, b. Nov. 4, 1905; married Clyde L. Stephens of Kansas City, Mo. (4) Mildred Rankin, b. Nov. 4, 1905—unmarried; was a twin of Marian.

This completes the data we have on the line of Captain William Alexander Rankin, father of Mrs. Lou Rankin Moore (Mrs. John T.) to whom we are greatly indebted for this data. Mrs. Moore resides in Bartlesville, Oklahoma.

We consider next the second child of Julia Doak Lowry:

2. ESTHER MONTGOMERY LOWRY, born Jan. 22, 1798, near Jonesboro, Washington county, Tennessee; she married Patric Carey, in 1818, and moved to Yorksville, South Carolina, where all of their children were born; they moved to Ripley, Ohio, in 1834; his wife died Jan. 16, 1891.

CHILDREN:—*Carey*.

(1) John C., b. Oct. 19, 1823; d. Dec. 22, 1893; married Oct. 10, 1850, Sarah B. Stephenson, of Bloomington, Illinois (she was b. Jan. 7, 1831—d. Apr. 20, 1898). They moved to Ripley, Ohio in 1834.

Children: (a) C. Edward Carey, b. June 29, 1864; d. Dec. 1, 1896; (b) Emma Carey;

(c) Anna Carey; (d) Alice Carey; and Robert Lee Carey.

(2) Samuel Doak Carey, b. July 21, 1830; married Martha Louise Fenton of Jamestown, New York, who died Dec. 1, 1888.

Children: (a) Eva Carey, married George C. Horton of Pasadena, Calif., and had two children, Mary Louise and Helen Clifford Horton, the latter married Joel Cox, of Wailuki, Maui, Ter Hawaii; (b) Charles Henry Carey, of Portland, Oregon; (c) Frank Niles; (d) Howard Fenton; (e) Forrest Woodard Carey of San Francisco, California.

(3) Lucinda Jane Carey, born Jan. 1, 1833.

(4) Mary Eliza Carey—twin of Lucinda—married in 1854 to Emmet Stallcup (d. 1865), they lived in South Indiana. She died at Ripley, Ohio, Sept. 4, 1907.

Children: (a) Sallie, b. Apr. 1, 1855, at Ripley, and married a Mr. Pierce, they had one son, William Pierce; (b) Lucy and Edward Stallcup.

(5) Edward Montgomery Carey, b. May 6, 1834; d. Sept. 1, 1884. Was a Captain of the first troops that left Ripley, Ohio (Civil War), he rose to the rank of Major and served with conspicuous gallantry until the close of the war. He was wounded in action and his brother was killed. He married Abigail Hill of Marietta, Ohio.

Children: (a) William K., b. Mar. 31, 1868; d. Nov. 5, 1897; (b) Julia Carey; (c) Harry Carey.

The third child of Julia Doak Lowry was:

3. REVEREND SAMUEL GARDNER LOWRY, who was born Mar. 26, 1800, in Washington county, Tennessee. He was a

son of Adam Lowry and Julia Doak Lowry. He was married first Nov. 16, 1820, to Almira Thompson, of Nicholas county, Kentucky, who was a daughter of James H. Thompson, one of the elders of the Concord Church in Nicholas county. We have no records of her mother. Her brother, Prof. S. H. Thompson, was for a long time connected with Hanover College, Indiana. Almira Thompson Lowry died April, 1828, and was buried at Kingston.

CHILDREN:—*Lowry*.

(1) Theophilus Lowry was a Presbyterian Minister. He went West early and settled in Freeborn county, Minnesota. He had a daughter who married a Mr. Sherwood. He also left a foster-son, Eugene Lowry, who resides in Moscow Township, Freeborn county—address Oakland, Minnesota.

(2) Samuel Doak Lowry was a teacher and settled in Texas. He had: David P.; Samuel Doak, Jr.; and Almira Lowry Laughlin of Texas.

(3) James Thompson Lowry was a physician in the Southern Army and died in California. He left no children.

(4) William Henry Lowry was a mechanic. He had: Julia Virginia; Annabel; Charles W.; Arthur; Doak; Frank; Fred; Eva and Mary Lowry.

All these four sons have been dead many years.

Reverend Samuel Gardner Lowry married for his second wife Maria Jane Hanna, of Hanover, Indiana, Feb. 26, 1829. She was a daughter of Samuel Hanna of Hanover.

Children by second wife:

(1) Almira Julia, died unm. about 1920, age 91 years.

(2) Felicia Lowry Morgan—died many years ago.

(3) Alfred Lowry—died 1922.

(4) Esther M. Lowry Dearmin—died 1917.
(5) Leander Chase Lowry—died 1917.
(6) Lucinda Anne Lowry is unm. and still living in Austin, Minnesota.
(7) Sarah Elizabeth Lowry was born in Putnam county, Indiana, June 17, 1832. She was married to William M. Catherwood on Nov. 9, 1854, and died in Austin, Minn., June, 1921, age 87.

CHILDREN:—*Catherwood.*

(a) Dr. Thomas Lowry Catherwood, born Aug. 9, 1856, in Putnam county, Ind., and died in Los Angeles, 1920. He married Jennie DeWolf of Cedar Rapids, Iowa, about 1890. She died about 1927.
Children: Bayard D. Catherwood of Los Angeles; Dorothy Alice Catherwood of Los Angeles; and Virginia Catherwood of Portland, Oregon.

(b) Samuel Doak Catherwood was born in Freeborn county, Minnesota, Nov. 12, 1859; married July 11, 1894, to Gertrude Sherwood of Austin, Minn. Judge Samuel Doak Catherwood continues his law practice at the age of 73. He is a member of the law firm of Catherwood, Hughes and Alderson of Austin, Minnesota. To him the author of this book is indebted for much valuable information, for which we wish to express our thanks.
Children: (1) Josephine Catherwood who married Robert Ely, and they have two children, Robert and Catherine Ely; (2) Roger Catherwood, who is practicing law with his father, and (3) Catherine Catherwood.

4. ELIZA ROWE LOWRY, born Jan. 10, 1808; married first Rev. Robert H. Rankin in 1833 at Ripley, Ohio. They afterwards moved to Crawfordsville, Indiana, where he died. She married second a Mr. Adams.

CHILDREN:—*Rankin.*
(1) Alexander, born Mar. 3, 1834.
(2) Mary Jane, born Nov. 13, 1836; lived at Osage, Kansas, and married William Thornton Merriwether.
(3) John Knox Rankin, born Nov. 3, 1838; died Oct., 1913.

5. MARY MERRIWETHER LOWRY was born in Washington county, Tennessee, June 6, 1810; died at Ft. Wayne, Indiana, July 20, 1841; she married at Felicity, Ohio, Oct. 26, 1829, to Reverend Alexander Taylor Rankin, son of Richard and Jane Steele Rankin. He was born near Dandridge, Tennessee, Dec. 4, 1803, and died at Baltimore, Md., Apr. 20, 1885. Dr. Rankin went to Denver, Colorado, from Buffalo, N. Y., in July, 1860, and left a most interesting diary in which he relates some of his impressions and experiences in "Denver City, close to the Rocky Mountains, Kansas Territory."

Dr. Rankin's great-granddaughter, Miss Helen Hine, is Librarian on a Denver newspaper and widely known in newspaper circles throughout the West.

CHILDREN:—*Rankin.*
(1) Sylvester Rankin, born June 26, 1831, in Felicity, Ohio; died May 22, 1881. He studied medicine at the University of Buffalo and graduated in 1859. At the beginning of the Civil War he entered the Union Army as a volunteer surgeon. Was with Kit Carson's Regiment, remained in service until the close of the war and was mentioned in dispatches for bravery several times. In July, 1865, he went into Mexico and served with the Mexican Army until July 19, 1867.

He married Feb. 8, 1879 at Victoria, Mexico, Francisco Garcia Y. Salizar. He was killed by bandits on the morning of May 22, 1881, as he was returning from visiting a sick patient. He left a daughter—Anna Mary Julia Rankin.

(2) Julia Rankin, born Oct. 11, 1835, in Felicity, Ohio; died 1928 in Denver, Colorado. She married Aug. 26, 1858, George Shaffer of Cumberland, Md. They had two children:
   (a) Annie Shaffer, married first Mr. Hine (or Hines) and married second Mr. Davenport. She had a son, also a daughter, Miss Helen Hine, who is a Librarian in Denver, Colorado.
   (b) Alexander Shaffer.

(3) William Rankin was born Apr. 6, 1838, at Fort Wayne, Indiana, when his father was the pastor of the First Presbyterian Church. He enlisted in the first regiment to leave Buffalo, N. Y., during the Civil War, was with the 21st New York Infantry. He married at Lockport, N. Y., June 6, 1865, to Mary Louise Wilson, born Mar. 17, 1848, at Newfane, N. Y.; died at Buffalo, N. Y., May 9, 1904, and was a daughter of Austin R. Wilson (b. Oct. 28, 1812—d. Aug. 20, 1894), of Acworth, N. H., and his wife, Miranda Olcott Wilson, of Stafford, N. Y., who was born June 29, 1820, and died July 9, 1909. William Rankin died in Buffalo, N. Y., Jan. 29, 1919.

CHILDREN :—*Rankin.*

   (a) Harriet M. Rankin.
   (b) Julia Rankin.
   (c) William A. Rankin, married Julia Wemirt, and they have one son—William G. Rankin.

The Doak Family

(d) Alexander T. Rankin, married Ethel Fero.

(e) Queenie F. Rankin, married B. A. Smith, and has two children—Kathleen and Burgus A. Smith, Jr.

(f) Mary Burt Rankin, of Buffalo, N. Y. To Miss Rankin the author of this book is greatly indebted for much valuable assistance in securing data. Miss Rankin is prominent in D. A. R. work, is a Colonial Dame, also active in Civic and club work.

(4) Thomas Bond Rankin, born Apr. 6, 1838.

The fifth child of Julia Doak Lowry was:

6. WILLIAM RAMSEY LOWRY, born Sept. 20, 1816; died Aug. 8, 1881; married first Evoline Manning of Felicity, Ohio. They had two sons—Walter and Theophilus.

CHILDREN:—*Lowry*.

(1) Walter Lowry, married Lucy Orr—*more later*.

(2) Theophilus Lowry—*more later*.

(3) Oswin Wells Lowry, married Clara K. Heyen —*more later*.

(4) Sarah Goodrich Lowry, m. Harris Crawford— *more later*.

(5) Julia Stevens Lowry, m. J. W. Keifer, Jr.— *more later*.

(6) Lucy Jean Lowry, married Frank S. Conn— *more later*.

(7) William Edward Lowry, born 1863—died 1870.

(8) Evoline Lowry, married Oliver D. Porter— *more later*.

(9) Katie Lowry, born 1870—died 1872.

(10) Charles Doak Lowry, married Lydia P. Hess —*more later*.

CHILDREN:—*Lowry*.

(1) Walter Lowry, married Lucy Orr, and had issue: Lucy, Lida, Cora, and a son, Cassius.

(2) Theophilus Lowry, was Color Corporal in Co. H, 12th Regiment, Ohio Volunteer Infantry, Civil War.

William Ramsey Lowry married second, Apr. 6, 1850, Rebekah Goodrich (b. Oct. 20, 1825), a daughter of Joseph Goodrich and Susan Stevens of Portland, Conn.

Children:

(3) Oswin Wells, b. 1852; d. 1898; married Clara K. Heyen. He was a lieutenant in the U. S. Navy.

(4) Sarah Goodrich, b. Aug. 27, 1854; M. Harris Crawford—see more later.

(5) Julia Stevens Lowry, born Oct. 15, 1856, in Ripley, Ohio; married Oct. 20, 1886, Joseph Warren Keifer, Jr., of Springfield, Ohio, a son of General Joseph Warren Keifer, and Eliza Stout. Mrs. Keifer, Jr., has rendered valuable assistance to the author of this Doak book in sending in data.

CHILDREN:—*Keifer*.

(a) Joseph William, b. Oct. 2, 1887. Was Top Sergeant in the World War, in France; married June 22, 1926, Thelma Amack, daughter of Ivan Amack, and Myrtle Holmgrain. They have one son: Joseph William Keifer, Jr., b. Aug. 17, 1927.

(b) Lucy Stout Keifer, b. Aug. 8, 1889; married June 12, 1923, John Ernest Bell, son of John D. Bell and Hulda Riggs Bell.

Children: John Ernest Bell, Jr., b. Dec.

21, 1925; Warren James Bell, b. Sept. 6, 1928, and Julia Evoline Bell, b. Sept. 16, 1931.

(c) Margaret Eliza Keifer, b. Apr. 1, 1891; married July 21, 1920, Joel Edward McLafferty, son of Fred S. McLafferty and Mary Hoagland.
Children: Lucy Grace, b. Nov. 22, 1921; Fred Warren, b. May 11, 1923; and Charles Lowry, b. Apr. 11, 1927.

(d) Oswin Keifer, b. July 26, 1893, was Lieutenant in France during the World War; married first Helen Kendall (dau. of Wallace and Lily Bradshaw Kendall), July 19, 1919; she died 1920, leaving a son, Oswin Keifer, Jr., b. Sept. 13, 1920. He married second Margaret Lang, Mar. 17, 1928, a daughter of John Lang and Eva Leonard Lang.

(6) Lucy Jean Lowry, born Jan. 11, 1859; married July 1, 1879, to Frank S. Conn (b. Apr. 4, 1853—d. Aug., 1893).

CHILDREN:—*Conn.*

(a) Julia Mabelle, b. May 28, 1881; married July 3, 1900, John Ellis Eyre (b. Aug. 26, 1873), son of Charles Eyre (b. Feb. 8, 1849) and Susan Palmer Eyre (b. Apr. 24, 1853).
Children: Delma Marguerita Eyre, b. Aug. 22, 1901, married June 7, 1922, to George McKinley Barber (b. Oct. 17, 1897), son of George Higley Barber of Massachusetts and Margaret Elizabeth Logan Barber (b. 1852).
Delma and George Barber have two children: Margaret Louise, b. Aug. 17, 1923, and John Philip Barber, b. Nov. 15, 1925.

Frances Eloise Eyre, b. Mar. 22, 1903; married Aug. 18, 1925, George Lawrence Whitney (b. July 29, 1898), a son of Byron Ephriam Whitney (b.) 1858—d. 1928), and Mary Rockwood Whitney (b. 1868—d. 1919). Frances and George Whitney have a son, George Lawrence Whitney, Jr., b. May 25, 1926.

Florence Rebekah Eyre, b. Jan. 15, 1905; married June 9, 1932, Philip Grant Koontz, son of Philip M. Koontz and Nancy Lee Koontz.

(b) Eunice Evoline Conn, born Jan. 13, 1883, unmarried.

(c) Lowry Laird Conn, born Oct. 30, 1884; married May 16, 1914, Alice Hasley. Children: Lowry Laird Conn, Jr., b. Jan. 28, 1915; Lucy Elizabeth Conn, b. Apr. 23, 1916; Malcolm William Conn, b. Jan. 6, 1918; Marion Conn, b. 1919.

(d) Doak Oswin Conn, born Sept. 20, 1888; died Nov. 16, 1917; married Elsa Herman, May 8, 1915, they had one son, Doak Oswin Conn, Jr., b. May 7, 1917.

(e) Warren Harris Conn, born June 22, 1892; died Dec. 16, 1893.

Mrs. Lucy Lowry Conn, the mother of the above children, is Librarian of the City Library, at Superior Nebraska. She is the sixth child of William Ramsey Lowry. His seventh child was:

(7) William Edward Lowry, born 1862—died 1870.

(8) Evoline Lowry, born 1868; married Oliver D. Porter, 1894, and had the following children:

(a) Samuel Doak Porter, b. 1896, married

Myrtle Reed and has Elinor and Donald Porter.
- (b) Elinor Porter, b. 1898, married Carl Erickson, and has Margaret, John and Robert Erickson.
- (c) Lowry Porter, b. 1900, married Miriam Fox.
- (d) James Porter, b. 1902.
- (e) Warren Porter, b. 1909.

(9) Katie Lowry, born 1870—died 1872.

(10) Charles Doak Lowry, born July 6, 1864; married June 28, 1895, Lydia Purdy Hess, daughter of George Henry Hess and Mary Howe Hess. Charles Doak Lowry received his A.B., A.M., from Northwestern University, and is now (1933) District Superintendent of Public Schools in the City of Chicago. We wish to extend to him our appreciation of assistance rendered in securing data for the Doak book.

Children:
- (a) Charles Doak Lowry, Jr., b. 1896; married 1922, Lucia Holmes (daughter of Wm. Elliott Holmes and Kate Hinman Holmes). They had a son, Charles Doak Lowry, III, who died in infancy.
- (b) Oswin William Lowry, b. 1900; married 1924, Sarah Huguenin (daughter of Philip Huguenin and Gertrude Bennet). They have a son, Oswin William, Jr., b. 1925, and Anne Lowry, b. 1929.
- (c) Louise Talman Lowry, born 1903.
- (d) Timothy Goodrich Lowry, b. 1905, married 1927, Katherine Bulkley, daughter of Charles C. and Lucy Williams Bulkley.
- (e) Oliver Howe Lowry, born 1910.

We continue with the line of William Ramsey Lowry, by giving that of his fourth child and daughter, Sarah Goodrich Lowry, who married Harris Crawford. This is rather a long line, hence was delayed until the last.

(4) SARAH GOODRICH LOWRY was born August 27, 1854; married Sept. 19, 1877, to Harris Crawford, who was born Oct. 23, 1848; died Mar. 4, 1928. Mrs. Harris Crawford resides at Pittsburgh, Pa.

CHILDREN:—*Crawford*.

(a) Oswin Lowry Crawford, born Dec. 21, 1879; married Gustava Karstorp (Nov. 12, 1882), June 10, 1907.
Children: Oswin Lowry Crawford, Jr., b. June 6, 1909; Eleanor Adelle Crawford, b. Apr. 1, 1911.

(b) Florence Maybelle Crawford, born Mar. 1, 1881; married Elgin A. Hill (b. Nov. 28, 1880), Oct. 19, 1904.
Children: E. Alexander Hill, Jr., b. Sept. 1, 1905; Florence Elizabeth Hill, b. May 20, 1913.

(c) Harris Weber Crawford, born Nov. 23, 1882; married Ruth Benbow (b. Mar. 12, 1890), June 17, 1916.
Children: Harris Weber Crawford, Jr., b. June 24, 1917; David Benbow Crawford, b. June 2, 1920.

(d) Clara Evoline Crawford, born June 4, 1884; died 1922; married Charles Mansfield Johnson (b. Mar., 1875—d. 1912), June 2, 1908.
Children: Florence Louise Johnson, b. Jan. 17, 1910; Charles Mansfield Johnson, Jr., b. June 6, 1912.

(e) Charles Goodrich Crawford, born May 4, 1886; married Winifred Pope (b. 1894), July, 1918.

Children: Josephine Crawford, b. May 24, 1920.
- (f) Frank Stevens Crawford, born Aug. 14, 1888; married Louise Kindle (b. 1895), in 1917.
 Children: Frances Louise Crawford, b. Mar. 7, 1919; Frank Stevens Crawford, Jr., b. Oct. 25, 1923.
- (g) Rebekah Irene Crawford, born Sept. 2, 1892; married Ralph Hastings Thomas (b. Apr. 27, 1891), June 28, 1917.
 Children: Ralph Hastings Thomas, Jr., b. July 25, 1918; John Taylor Thomas, b. July, 1922; Robert Harris Thomas, b. Apr. 3, 1927.
- (h) Sarah Grace Crawford, born Aug. 24, 1894; married Ian Forbes (b. 1892), Sept. 23, 1918.
 Children: Ian Forbes, Jr., b. Jan. 16, 1920; Jean Forbes, b. Aug. 23, 1923; Betty Ann Forbes, b. Apr. 1, 1925.

This completes our records of the line of Julia Doak Lowry's son, William Ramsey Lowry. We now take the line of her daughter:

7. LUCINDA LOWRY, who was born about 1818; married William McNish, of Ripley, Ohio; they had four sons and four daughters. We have records of the following:

CHILDREN :—*McNish.*

- (1) James H. McNish was a soldier in the Civil War—Co. H, 12th Regt., Ohio Volunteer Infantry; he died from the effects of the war, in Ripley, Ohio, June 13, 1863.
- (2) James K. McNish was a Corporal in Co. H, 12th Regt., Ohio Volunteer Infantry—Civil War—died in action.
- (3) Julia McNish married John Courtney. Children: Carrie, Nellie, Lida, and Dottie Courtney.

(4) William McNish married Laura O'Connelly.

Children: Ottie and Harvey McNish, of St. Paul, Minnesota.

All of the McNish family records were burned. The "McNish Cellar" of the McNish building, was the first station of the "underground railroad" for hiding slaves who escaped from or through Kentucky. The second station was on the hill just back of Ripley, Ohio, at the home of Rev. John Rankin, whose wife was Jean Lowry, sister of the above Mrs. Lucinda Lowry McNish. It was in the home of Mrs. Jean Lowry Rankin that Harriett Beecher Stowe got much of her data for "Uncle Tom's Cabin."

This completes the line of Julia Doak Lowry.

Of Rev. Samuel Doak's two sons we have the following:

I. REVEREND JOHN WHITFIELD DOAK.

John Whitfield Doak was born October 18, 1778, in Augusta county, Virginia; he married 1809, Jane H. Alexander, who was a sister of Rev. Archibald Alexander of Princeton Theological College. She was born in Rockbridge county, Virginia.

John W. Doak was educated under his father's tutelage and licensed to preach by the Abingdon Presbytery when he was nineteen and shortly thereafter was ordained and installed pastor of New Dublin and Wytheville Churches in Southwest Virginia. He was subsequently pastor of Mount Bethel and Providence Churches in Tennessee. In the year 1809 he was installed pastor of the church in Frankfort, Pennsylvania.

In consequence of the failure of his health, which rendered it doubtful whether he would be able to continue in the ministry, he studied medicine—returned to Tennessee and became a very successful practitioner and at the same time he officiated as a supply of Salem and Leesburgh Churches.

He was Vice-President of Washington College in 1806, and remained in that office until his departure for Pennsylvania in 1809. In 1818 he was elected President of Washington College to succeed his father, who had resigned, and remained President until his death—October 6, 1820.

CHILDREN:—*Doak.*

1. Samuel Harvey Doak, married Elizabeth Galbreath, and had issue:
    (1) John Doak.
    (2) Joseph Doak.
    (3) Beesher Doak.
    (4) Dr. Wiley Harvey Doak, who married Katherine Nenney, and their daughter, Elizabeth, married Rev. Benjamin David Kennedy.

Genealogy of the Reverend Samuel Doak, D.D. 39

2. James Witherspoon Doak. No records.
3. Sophia Doak. No records.
4. Eliza Smith Doak, married Dr. Bovelle; he had a daughter by his first wife, who married Rev. Samuel (?) Hodge.
5. Jane Doak, married Ezekiel Mathis, and had a son, Ezekiel Mathis, Jr.
6. Esther Montgomery Doak, married William W. Bovelle or Bevelle, who died Aug. 10, 1835.
7. Mary Doak, married William Smithpeters. The name of this daughter is not mentioned in the will of John W. Doak, but was sent in by a descendant who knows that she was a daughter.
8. Archibald Alexander Doak—see more later.
9. John Newton Doak—see more later.

8. REVEREND ARCHIBALD ALEXANDER DOAK.

Reverend Archibald Alexander Doak was born July 13, 1815, in Pennsylvania, while his father was pastor at Frankfort. He was President of Washington College from 1840 to 1856, and again from 1852 to 1856.

He married Sarah Paxton Cowan, daughter of John Cowan and Sarah Paxton Cowan of Leesburg, Tennessee. Sarah Paxton was a daughter of John Paxton and Sarah Walker of Rockbridge county, Virginia, and a sister of Rev. John Paxton, D.D., of Kentucky.

Children:—*Doak*.

(1) Henry Melville Doak—see more later.
(2) James Hall Doak—unmarried; died in the Confederate Army in 1862.
(3) Samuel Taylor Coleridge Doak, unmarried.
(4) William Edmonson Kennedy Doak—see more later.
(5) Sarah Jane Doak, died young.

The Doak Family

(6) Mabel Doak, died young.
(7) Saba Doak, see more later.
(8) Algernon Sidney Doak, see more later.
(9) John Newton Doak, see more later.

(1) HENRY MELVILLE DOAK, born Aug. 3, 1841; was Editor of the Nashville American, also Cincinnati News and Memphis Avalanche. He was Clerk of the United States Court for forty-two years, and at his death was succeeded by his son, E. Lockert Doak, of Nashville, Tenn. At the time of his death, Sept. 28, 1928, he had served as Deputy Sheriff for 39 years. He was in the Confederate Army, also Navy; received his parole at Appomattox, Va., Apr. 10, 1865. He wrote many articles on "Memories of American Stage" and "Confederate War Days." He was considered one of the best informed men of the South. He was a friend of Booth and was asked by him for criticism on his acting of Hamlet.

He married Margaret Lockert of Clarksville, Tennessee, who also was very brilliant, and wrote for "Shakespearana," and organized a Shakespeare Club in Nashville, Tenn.

CHILDREN:—

(a) Margaret Lacy Doak.
(b) Archibald Alexander Doak—more later.
(c) Elias Lockert Doak, a prominent lawyer of Nashville, also holds the clerkship that his father held in U. S. Federal Court. He married Maude Moore and they have one son, Elias Lockert Doak, Jr.
(d) Henry Melville Doak, Jr., deceased—was an Annapolis student and a young man of rare charm.

(b) Archibald Alexander Doak is an engineer with the Nashville Water System. He married Bess Thuss, whose father was a very prominent photographer in Nashville for over fifty years.

Bess Thuss was born and reared in Nashville—is a graduate of Ward Seminary, class of 1899; she also took a special course at Fairmont Seminary in Washington, D. C. She is an active club woman—having been Vice-President of Tennessee Congress of Parent-Teachers, and is now on the Board of Tennessee Federation of Woman's Clubs, and also has served as president of League of Women Voters; member of the Tennessee Woman's Press and Authors Club.

They have no children.

(4) WILLIAM EDMONSON KENNEDY DOAK (son of Rev. A. A. Doak), was born March 15, 1857, in Washington county, Tenn., and married Emma L. Wilson, daughter of James H. Wilson of Nashville, Tenn. W. E. K. Doak was in the newspaper work.

CHILDREN:—

(a) Henry Melville Doak, of Jackson, Miss., married Susie Gray of Nashville, Tenn.

(b) Samuel Gordon Doak, a civil engineer of Nashville, married Anice Turner and has one son, William Melville Doak, born Mar. 21, 1930.

(c) Felix Zollicoffer Doak of Dothan, Alabama, they have two daughters, Margaret Louise and Shirley Doak. He married Louise Spichard of Nashville, Tenn.

(d) Virginia Paxton Doak, married Darwin A. Hindman, and resides at Columbus, Ohio.

(7) SABA DOAK (dau. of Rev. A. A. Doak), was born Apr. 21, 1856; died Jan. 8, 1898; married Benjamin Shaw, of Montgomery county, on Oct. 20, 1881; reside at Clarksville, Tennessee.

CHILDREN:—*Shaw*.

(a) John William Shaw, born Sept. 18, 1882; married Bernice Smithson.

The Doak Family

(b) Margaret Doak Shaw, born Nov. 7, 1884; married Aug. 20, 1913, to Alfred Ewin Anderson, son of Frank O. and Susie Ewin Anderson. Issue: Alfred Ewin, Jr., born Oct. 2, 1914; Margaret Josephine, b. Dec. 7, 1916; Susie Ewin, b. May 22, 1918—died Nov., 1918.

(c) Henry Sidney Shaw, born Apr. 1, 1886; married Mrs. Lillian (Roberts) Slayden.

(d) Thomas Benjamin Shaw, born Feb. 16. 1888—deceased.

(e) Josephine Fizer Shaw, born July 31, 1890.

(f) Helen Shaw, twin of Josephine, died Aug., 1890.

(8) REVEREND ALGERNON SIDNEY DOAK (son of Rev. A. A. Doak), was born Sept. 10, 1846, in Washington county, Tennessee; married Dec. 26, 1878, at Petersburg, Virginia, to Emma Regina Smith, daughter of Jacob Smith (b. June 9, 1853), of New Market, Tenn., and later of Bluff City, Tenn., where he died. Jacob Smith was for many years a Ruling Elder in the Presbyterian Church at New Market.

CHILDREN:—*Doak.*

(a) Saba Regina Doak, born Oct., 1879, in Texas. Deceased.

(b) Flora Paxton Doak, born Nov., 1881, in Texas; married Dr. Frank Wilson, of Huntsville, Alabama. Issue: William Doak Wilson; Frank Beatty Wilson; and Hugh Wilson.

(c) Sidney Smith Doak; wife deceased; left one child, Emma Ann Doak, of Knoxville, Tennessee.

(d) Delia Katherine Doak, unmarried. Miss Doak is prominent both in the social and business life of Huntsville, Ala.; is a partner in the "Liliputian Shoppe."

(e) Edward Wzelle Doak, married Dixie Denton.

(f) Hugh Keffer Doak, married Elizabeth Murray, daughter of W. R. Murray, of Huntsville, Ala.; they have one son, Hugh Keffer Doak, Jr.

(g) Alexander Cowan, married but has no children.

SKETCH OF REV. A. S. DOAK.

Reverend Algernon Sidney Doak (son of Rev. A. A. Doak) now resides in Huntsville, Alabama, with his daughter, Mrs. Frank Wilson, and Dr. Wilson. He is a retired Presbyterian Minister after giving the best years of his life in active service. He is the fourth minister in direct line of descent from the pioneer Minister, the Reverend Samuel Doak.

Rev. A. S. Doak was in the War Between the States, during which time he served as Midshipman in the Confederate States Navy, 1863-1865. He was thirty years of age when he entered the ministry—having spent three years in Union Theological Seminary in Virginia, graduating there on Dec. 26, 1878; was ordained by the Holston Presbytery of Tennessee. Shorty thereafter he went to Texas where he was engaged in missionary work from the Fall of 1876 until the Fall of 1885. His first charge was at Weatherford, Texas. Other fields of labor were: Valley Creek Church, in the Presbytery of Tuscaloosa, Alabama; Alabama Avenue Church, at Selma, Ala.; resigned from this charge on account of ill health—malaria—and engaged in Home Mission Work in and around Birmingham, Ala., for about one year. His next charge was in Jefferson City, Tennessee, and White Pine Church, Tenn. From there he went to Kingston and Waccamaw Churches in South Carolina, where he remained seven years. His last charge was at Roswell and Norcross, Georgia, in the Presbytery of Atlanta. While there he reached his 70th birthday—the age of retirement.

The Presbytery of Atlanta put him on the Honorably Retired Roll. Even though he is retired and 85 years old, Rev. A. Sidney Doak has a live and interesting Sunday School Class in his home town—Huntsville, Alabama.

Well has he carried the NAME—*Doak*, and SERVICES —*Minister*, down through the ages.

This completes our records of the line of Rev. Archibald Alexander Doak (son of Rev. John Whitfield Doak). We next give the line of his other son:

(9) JOHN NEWTON DOAK.

John Newton Doak, son of Reverend John Whitfield Doak, was born in 1812 and died in 1881; married Emily George (b. 1822—d. 1889), Jan. 2, 1838. She was a daughter of Robert George and Susan Lacy George.

CHILDREN :—*Doak*.

(1) Thomas J. Doak.
(2) Robert D. Doak.
(3) John Newton Doak, Jr.
(4) Martha E. Doak.
(5) Annie F. Doak, married a Mr. Bailey.
(6) Mary H. Doak, married J. J. Davis.
(7) Thankful Caroline Doak.

THANKFUL CAROLINE DOAK was born 1845 and died 1892; married Hugh Lawson Preston (b. 1841—d. 1919), son of William B. Preston and Mary Mears Preston, and a grandson of Thomas Preston.

CHILDREN :—*Preston*.

(a) William Doak Preston, born 1866 and died 1926, was a farmer. He married Dovie Cummings and had issue: Katherine, who married Robert Gray, and Walter Preston.

(b) Thomas Ross Preston, born 1868. Is President of the Hamilton National Bank, of Chattanooga, Tennessee. He was president of the American Bankers Association in 1928; and is prominently connected with civic and industrial affairs of that city. During the World War, Mr. Preston was a dollar-a-year man; was in charge of the Liberty Loan Campaign, and for the last thirteen months of the war was Director of War Savings for Tennessee, and at the close of the war he was made chairman of the Agricultural Commission of the War Finance Corporation of Tennessee, North Georgia, and North Alabama.

He married June 5, 1895, Roberta Clift, daughter of Col. Moses H. Clift (lawyer) and Charlotte A. Cooke Clift, and granddaughter of Col. William Clift and Nancy Arwin Brooks Clift—whose ancestor, Moses Brooks, was a Lieutenant in Virginia Militia.

Mrs. Preston is equally as prominent as her distinguished husband; is actively engaged in the various clubs and organizations of the city, namely: Daughters of the American Revolution, Daughters of the Confederacy, the Junior League, Kosmos-Woman's Club.

Mr. and Mrs. Thomas Ross Preston have two children: Arwin Clift Preston, born 1902; married first, Knapp Milburn; married second, Wilbur Seymour Lawson, Aug. 18, 1927. Thomas Ross Preston, Jr., born 1905; married Sept. 1, 1931, Martha Merriam, daughter of Isaac and Ethel Bell Merriam.

Mr. and Mrs. Lawson have a daughter, Roberta Jane Lawson, born 1933; and Mr. and Mrs. Thomas Ross Preston,

THE DOAK FAMILY

Jr., have a son, Thomas Ross Preston, III, born 1933.

(c) Mina Preston, born 1870; married Albert M. Dement, and has a daughter, Huda Dement.

(d) Charles Miller Preston, born 1874. Unmarried. Is President of the Hamilton National Bank of Knoxville, Tennessee, and Vice-President of the Hamilton National Bank of Chattanooga, Tennessee.

(e) John White Preston, born 1877. Was United States District Attorney at San Francisco, California, during the World War, and later was made a Special Assistant Attorney General of the United States, and is now Justice of the Supreme Court of California. He married Jane Rucker.
Children: Elizabeth Preston married Robert Hatch, and has Robert Hatch, Jr., and John White Preston, Jr.

(f) Hugh Lawson Preston, born 1881; married Florence Rudduck, of California. They have a son, Hugh Lawson Preston, Jr. For a number of years Mr. Preston was Judge of the Supreme Court of California, and is now the Presiding Justice of Appellate Court of California.

(g) Howard Payne Preston, born 1886; married Effie Case, of California. They have issue: Virginia and Marjory Preston. Mr. Preston is a Banker, and Vice-President of the Trans-American Company of New York.

This completes our records on the line of Rev. Samuel Doak's oldest son—Rev. John Whitfield Doak.

We next consider the line of his younger son—Rev. Samuel Witherspoon Doak.

II. REVEREND SAMUEL WITHERSPOON DOAK.

Samuel Witherspoon Doak, the second son of Rev. Samuel Doak, D. D., was born March 24, 1785, and died Feb. 3, 1864. He was president of each of the schools founded by his father; president of Washington College from 1838 to 1840, and in 1842 he became president of Tusculum College, where he remained until his death about the close of the war. He is buried at Mount Bethel, Greeneville, Tennessee.

He married March 3, 1808, his step-sister, Sarah Houston McEwen (b. June 17, 1792), a daughter of Alexander and Margaretta (Houston) McEwen.

CHILDREN:—*Doak.*

1. Samuel Smith McEwen Doak, b. Mar. 7, 1809. More later.
2. Esther Montgomery Doak, born and died in 1811.
3. John Keith Doak, born and died in 1813.
4. John Whitfield Doak, b. Sept. 14, 1814. More later.
5. Eliza F. R. Doak, born Feb. 22, 1817, in Finley, Ohio; married Dr. Mathew Gibson.
6. Alexander Mason Doak, b. Mar. 26, 1819. More later.
7. Robert Ely Janeway Doak, born 1821; died 1823.
8. Robert Ebenezer Doak, b. Mar. 4, 1824. More later.
9. Mary Jane Doak, born July 14, 1826; married Robert Cox.
10. William Stephenson Doak, b. Mar. 27, 1829. More later.
11. Juila Margaretta Doak, b. Feb. 19, 1832. More later.
12. Matthew Stephenson Doak, b. Feb. 13, 1835. More later.
13. Lourinda Cutter Doak, b. Apr. 12, 1838. More later.

1. DR. SAMUEL SMITH MCEWEN DOAK, was born March 7, 1809; died June 4, 1883. He was a prominent physician of Rhea county, Tennessee, and served as a surgeon in Captain Darling A. Wild's Company in the Seminole War, and he also served with the United States Troops

which accompanied the Cherokee Indians to the West, and was Surgeon in the War Between the States. He married Eliza Diana Snapp (b. 1806—d. 1878) in 1830. Dr. and Mrs. Doak are listed with Chattanooga's "53 First Citizens." They lived near Soddy, Tenn., in Rhea county, where he purchased 5,000 acres of land on Roaring Creek, on March 26, 1834; they joined the Soddy Presbyterian Church June 19, 1836. A short time after that date they moved to Ross's Landing, which is now Chattanooga, Tennessee.

CHILDREN:—*Doak.*

1. William Clay Doak. More later.

2. John Valentine Doak, died in the Confederate Army.

3. Sarah Diana Doak, born 1836; married her cousin, Samuel Doak.

4. Samuel Snapp Doak, born 1832. More later.

1. WILLIAM CLAY DOAK, married Mary Van Huss, and had Kate and Sarah Etta Doak.

    (1) Sarah Etta Doak, born May 26, 1869; married Daniel C. Morris, May 26, 1887. The old Morris plantation is now the present site of Morristown, Tennessee, which was named for the founder—the father of Daniel C. Morris.

CHILDREN:—*Morris.*

    (a) Katie Sue Morris, born Mar. 4, 1888; married Robert McHargue, Aug. 11, 1911; they have two children: Robert, Jr., and David S. McHargue.

    (b) James Morris, born May 26, 1892.

    (c) Maria Morris, born Sept. 26, 1895; died 1921; married Dr. Paul Henderson, Mar. 27, 1915, and have a son, Paul Henderson, Jr., born June 14, 1916.

    (d) Daniel C. Morris, Jr., born 1899—died 1901.

- (e) George Morris, born Mar. 15, 1904.
- (f) Mabel Doak Morris, born 1890; married Prof. Samuel T. Schroetter, director of music at Virginia Intermont College, Bristol, Virginia. They have one child, Samuel T. Schroetter, Jr., who is keenly interested in the history of his famous ancestor, the Reverend Samuel Doak, D.D.

  Mrs. Schroetter has a set of teaspoons that belonged to Rev. Samuel Doak and his wife, Esther Montgomery Doak, which are marked "S. & E. D." She also has his old reading lamp, made of iron with a place for the wick to hang over out of the oil. It has a hook to hang over the ladder-back chair, and was his own personal reading lamp. She also has some of his orig'nal sermon manuscripts.

4. PROF. SAMUEL SNAPP DOAK, was born 1832 and died 1872. He was educated for and practiced law, but later succumbed to the Doak lure, teaching, and became a professor of mathematics and Vice-President of Hiwassee College. After the death of his grandfather—Rev. Samuel Witherspoon Doak—he was prevailed upon to go to Tusculum College in the same capacity. He, almost alone, kept the college in operation during the war period (War Between the States).

He died at Tusculum in 1872; he married in 1857, Julia Marianna King, who was born Mar. 12, 1824, and died Mar. 8, 1896.

CHILDREN:—*Doak.*

- (1) Mabel Doak, born Jan. 18, 1859—died 1879.
- (2) Samuel King Doak, born 1860—died 1869.
- (3) Bertha Doak, married Dr. J. W. Stewart, in 1896.

(4) Dr. Hubert P. Doak, born Feb. 29, 1864; died Feb. 5, 1911; married Harriet Armitage, a sister of James Armitage of Greeneville, Tennessee, who was the father of Mrs. James A. Stone (Irene Armitage) of Bristol, Virginia. Mrs. James A. Armitage makes her home with her daughter, Mrs. Stone, also spends several weeks out of each year with her sons in Greeneville, Tennessee.

Mrs. Hubert P. Doak (Harriet Armitage) resides at the old homestead near Tusculum College and has the following children:

(a) Prof. Samuel Armitage Doak, born 1894; married Mary Lawall in 1925; they have a son Samuel L. Doak, born Mar. 31, 1928, and is the NINTH Samuel Doak in direct line.

(b) Harriet Alpha Armitage Doak, born 1896; married Claude Russell in 1927.

(c) Maurice Stewart Armitage Doak, born 1898; married Gertrude Bailey Lichens in 1929.

(d) Bertha Armitage Doak, born 1900; married George Sipple in 1924; they have a daughter, Harriet Ann Sipple, born Jan. 30, 1929.

(5) Maude Doak, born Aug. 19, 1869; married Sept. 25, 1889, to Charles E. Coile (b. June 14, 1868) of Greeneville, Tennessee. The author of this book is greatly indebted to both Mr. and Mrs. Coile for their most valuable assistance in compiling genealogical data—for which we wish to extend our thanks. Mrs. Coile is a prominent member of the Presbyterian Church, also an active W.C.T.U. worker, as well as prominent in political government. She is an outstanding member of the D.A.R.—wearing three

GENEALOGY OF THE REVEREND SAMUEL DOAK, D.D. 51

bars on her D.A.R. ribbon—one of them being for the patriotic services of Rev. Samuel Doak.

CHILDREN :—*Coile.*

(a) Merrill Doak Coile, born Nov. 19, 1891; married Margaret Harrington, Nov. 13, 1923; they have issue: Martha Delane, born 1926; Charles Harrington, born 1928; Carolyn Louise, born 1930.

(b) Eugene Leland Coile, born Feb. 13, 1895; married Grace Anna Armstrong, Dec. 15, 1923.

Mr. and Mrs. Coile also rendered valuable assistance in compiling genealogical data for the Doak book. They have an attractive little daughter, Anna Armstrong Coile, born May 29, 1928.

(c) Charles Eric Coile, born June 22, 1896; died June 27, 1904.

(5) Reverend Maurice J. Doak, youngest son of Prof Samuel Snapp Doak, was born 1870 and died unmarried in 1899.

This ends the line of Dr. Samuel Smith McEwen Doak. We next take that of his brothers.

4. JOHN WHITFIELD KEITH DOAK, was born Sept. 14, 1814; died May 28, 1891; married Margaret West. He built a residence at Tusculum after his marriage and lived there for some time—later removing to Tunnel Hill, Georgia. He sold this home and sixty acres of land to his brother, Rev. William S. Doak, who lived there until his death. Later his widow and children conveyed the greater part of this land to Tusculum College and part of the family moved to New York. The original home of J. W. K. Doak is now occupied by one of the professors of Tusculum College.

CHILDREN :—*Doak.*

(1) Richard West Doak, married Laura Ponder.

(2) Edward William Doak.
(3) Sarah Doak.
(4) Mary Lou Doak, married William Mathes.
(5) Mattie Emmons Doak, married Jay Humphrey.
(6) Luther Doak.

6. ALEXANDER MASON DOAK, was born March 26, 1819; died Aug. 22, 1903; married first, Eliza McClure, Aug. 9, 1844; married second, Hattie McLin Carmack; no issue by second marriage.

CHILDREN:—*Doak*.

(1) James McClure Doak, born April 14, 1845; died at Camp Douglas during the War Between the States.
(2) Sarah Ann Eilza Doak, born Oct. 2, 1846; died Aug. 14, 1912; married William Kite.
(3) Susan Virginia Doak, born Apr. 14, 1848; died July 25, 1916
(4) Samuel Houston Doak, born Jan. 22, 1851; died Nov. 4, 1921.
(5) Mary Augusta Doak, born May 30, 1853; married Jesse Morrison.
(6) Eudora Elmira Doak, born Dec. 14, 1854; died Feb. 4, 1920; married W. C. Wells (died Feb. 11, 1913), and have two children, Doak and Sue Wells.
(7) Alice Florida Doak, born Feb. 1, 1857; married Frank McNutt, and they have James and Mary McNutt.
(8) Robert Horace Doak, born Jan. 17, 1859; died May 26, 1928; married 1896, Cleo White, who was born Mar. 25, 1871.
CHILDREN:—
(a) Hannah Eliza Doak, born Apr. 6, 1899. We wish to extend our thanks to "Miss Hannah" for her part in making

this Doak book more complete by compiling this line of Alexander Mason Doak.

(b) Ruby Oatman Doak, born Mar. 8, 1901. Both Miss Ruby and Miss Hannah Doak reside in Johnson City, Tennessee.

(c) Lucile Callahan Doak, born Feb. 9, 1904 —died 1909.

(d) Stanley Alexander Doak, born Apr. 4, 1906; married June 9, 1926, Nellie Campbell, and they have: Charlotte Lee, b. June 19, 1927; Joan Christine, b. Dec., 1928, and Robert Campbell Doak, b. Mar. 1, 1931.

(e) Samuel Kitz Miller Doak, born Oct. 28, 1910.

8. ROBERT EBENEZER DOAK (son of Rev. S. W. Doak), was born March 4, 1824; died 1865; married Anna Kate Kreger (b. 1830).

CHILDREN:—*Doak*.

(1) Cynthia Anne Houston Doak, married John Snibley, and have issue: Harriet and Doak Snibley.

(2) Mary Katharine Doak, married Lacy L. Lawrence, and have issue: Fred, Minnie Lee, and Maud Willis Lawrence, who married Dr. Marks and they have Virginia and Lawrence Marks.

(3) Oliver Doak, died in infancy.

(4) Margaret Ellen Doak, died in infancy.

(5) Henry Randolph Doak, unmarried.

(6) Sarah Virginia, married Newton Sloan and had issue: Robert Doak; Mary Katherine; Bessie; Clyde; Edward and Lee Sloan.

10. REVEREND WILLIAM STEPHENSON DOAK (son of Rev. S. W. Doak), was born March 27, 1829; died May 23, 1882; married Fannie Banton. He, too, was educated for the medical profession, but soon felt the "Doak urge" and became a Minister of the Gospel. He succeeded his father, Rev. Samuel Witherspoon Doak, as president of Tusculum College.

CHILDREN:—*Doak.*

(1) Julia Doak, died 1929; married a Mr. Tabor —no issue.

(2) John Doak, married Anna Bell Gass—no issue.

(3) Robert Doak, married Floy Folger, and had issue: Frances and Banton Doak.

(4) William Doak, died at age of 21.

(5) Edward Doak, married Susie ———?

(6) Nellie Doak.

(7) Randolph Doak, unmarried.

11. JULIA MARGARETTA DOAK (dau. of Rev. S. W. Doak), was born Feb. 19, 1832; married Dr. William Samuel Anderson.

CHILDREN:—*Anderson.*

(1) Mary Jane Anderson.

(2) William Coleman Anderson, of Newport, Tenn., a Congressman, who married Blanche Gouchenour, and have issue:

(a) Julia Blanche Anderson.

(b) Herbert Gouchenour Anderson.

(c) Margaret Elizabeth Anderson.

(d) Robert Doak Anderson.

(e) Mary Louise Anderson.

(f) William Cowan Anderson.

(g) Jean Olive Anderson.

(3) Samuel Doak Newman Anderson, married Margaret Wilson, and had issue:
  (a) Samuel Wilson Anderson, married first, Kate ————; married second, Wilhemenia ————?
  (b) Fain Anderson.
  (c) Joseph Smith Anderson.
  (d) John Anderson.
  (e) Charles Anderson.
  (f) Dora Anderson.
  (g) Leslie Anderson.
  (h) Alexander Anderson.
(4) Sarah Lourinda Anderson, unmarried, resides in Johnson City, Tenn.
(5) Smith Pleasant Anderson, died 1884.
(6) Joseph James Anderson, died 1884.
(7) Julia Emma Anderson, unmarried, resides in Johnson City, Tenn.
(8) Alexander Eckel Anderson.
(9) Josephine Houston Anderson, married W. A. Campbell.

12. DR. MATTHEW STEPHENSON DOAK (son of Rev. S. W. Doak), was born Feb. 13, 1835; died Oct. 23, 1883; married Margaret Kreger in 1857.

CHILDREN:—*Doak.*

(1) Frank Orlando Doak, born 1861—died 1879.
(2) Charles Smith Doak, born Sept. 4, 1859; married Oct. 11, 1892, Lucinda Thompson, who was born Nov. 4, 1865. Mr. Charles S. Doak is now residing in the old brick home built by his ancestor, the Reverend Samuel Doak, D.D., over 100 years ago. Just "a stone's throw" distance is a little log cabin

THE DOAK FAMILY

—remains of the first Tusculum Academy, across which are thrown the shadows from modern brick structures including the fine new administration building of Tusculum College, which was dedicated in 1928. Mr. Doak graduated from Tusculum 50 years ago.

Mr. Doak has in his possession some of the personal effects of his ancestor, namely: his hat, powder horn, measure for a load of powder, seal, diploma from Princeton in 1775 (two names on it were signers of the Declaration of Independence, viz. John Witherspoon, and Robert Morris), a drinking cup made from leather, and deeds to land dated 1782, State of North Carolina; his watch and his secretary which is now (1933) 123 years old. Their children were:

(a) Margaret Lee Doak, born Aug. 10, 1893; married Delfido Cardova, Aug. 10, 1916. He is a Spaniard whom she met in Mexico. She died in 1918, leav'ng a son, Carlos King Cardova, born June 27, 1917, who was adopted by his grandparents, Mr. and Mrs. Charles Smith Doak. He is a student at Tusculum which was established and maintained by his distinguished ancestors.

(b) Lawrence Thompson Doak, born Jan. 26, 1903—died 1903.

(c) Harry Lynn Doak, twin of Lawrence, also died 1903.

13. LOURINDA CUTTER DOAK (dau. of Rev. S. W. Doak), was born Apr. 12, 1838; died Nov. 9, 1904; married first, William R. Ramsey, Aug. 8, 1856 (he was b. Dec. 23, 1835—died Aug. 8, 1862); she married second, Thomas Alexander —no issue by second marriage.

CHILDREN:—*Ramsey*.

(1) Wilberforce Alexander Ramsey, born June 18, 1857; died 1931; married first, Frances Feemster; married second, Effie Keeble, in 1888. Had issue:

    (a) Winnifred Ramsey.

    (b) Wilbur Ramsey, died 1918 in the World War.

    (c) Ruth Ramsey.

    (d) Julia Ramsey.

(2) Samuel Doak Ramsey, born Aug. 29, 1859; died Mar. 2, 1929; married Ollie Bates and had issue:

    (a) Raymond Ramsey, married a Miss White.

    (b) Robert Ramsey, died at age of 12 years.

    (c) Roy Ramsey.

    (d) Prof. Hugh Trent Ramsey, of Lincoln Memorial University, married Helen Anderson.

    (e) Samuel Doak Ramsey, Jr., resides in New York.

    (f) Louise Ramsey, married Prof. Frank Alexander, Aug. 11, 1931, who is a cousin of Prof. Fred Alexander, former president of Stonewall Jackson College, at Abingdon, Virginia.

(3) Willoughby Francis Ramsey, born Dec. 7, 1861; unmarried; died Oct. 9, 1884, at Raleigh, North Carolina.

This completes our genealogical data on the line of the pioneer preacher and teacher—the Reverend Samuel Doak, D.D. We feel sure there are many more descendants who could have given us valuable data had we been able to get in touch with them. Our method of securing even this much has been "from hand to mouth"—different ones telling of still others.

For a sketch of the life of Reverend Samuel Doak, D.D., see Chapter IV.

Chapter III
OTHER DOAK LINES

SOME DOAK LINES WE WERE UNABLE TO CONNECT WITH
REVEREND SAMUEL DOAK, D.D.

DOAK FAMILY OF WILSON COUNTY, LEBANON, TENNESSEE.

By

RUFUS RANDOLPH DOAK.

"My great-grandfather was JOHN DOAK, who married Polly Foster July 11, 1793; their son, JOHN FOSTER DOAK, was born April 28, 1801; married Colie Harrison; they had four sons and two daughters:

1. William H. Doak.
2. Rufus Preston Doak.
3. John Foster Doak, Jr.
4. Andrew Jackson Doak.

All four sons were in the War Between the States; Rufus was killed at the battle of Manassas, Virginia; the other three have since died.

5. Mary Doak, unmarried.
6. Bettie Doak, married a Mr. Elliott—no issue.

Both these daughters are dead.

"My father was JOHN FOSTER DOAK, JR., who was born

Buena Vista Langford, who survives him; they had three sons:

(1) Rufus Randolph Doak, of Lebanon, Tennessee.
(2) Samuel Langford Doak, of Portland, Oregon.
(3) Ervin Foster Doak, of Lebanon, Tennessee.

"John Foster Doak (my grandfather) was tendered the cabinet position of Secretary of the United States Treasury, by President James K. Polk, during his administration. He declined to accept for reason he never aspired or desired to hold political office, preferring to live a quiet life on his farm in Wilson county, near Lebanon, Tennessee. While never seeking an office, he was always very active and influential in county, state and National politics. He was a man of very strong character, unquestionable integrity, and was a natural born leader of men during his day. So much so that it was a common expression in elections: 'However Foster Doak votes, so does Wilson county.' He died in 1882 at the age of 82, on his farm near Lebanon, Tennessee."

Mr. Rufus Randolph Doak, who compiled this sketch of his family, is with the AMERICAN INSURANCE COMPANY, of New Jersey, and resides at Lebanon, Tennessee.

While we are unable to connect this line with that of the Rev. Samuel Doak, we find the name "Randolph" among the line of his two sons, Rev. John Whitfield Doak and Rev. Samuel Witherspoon Doak. If any reader can assist us in this matter please write Mr. Rufus Randolph Doak, Lebanon, Tenn., or Mrs. J. Stewart French, Birmingham, Alabama.

DOAK FAMILY OF KENTUCKY,

BY

DR. JAMES W. BLACKBURN, of Bowling Green.

I. ——— Doak.

His son:

II. Alexander Doak, born July 18, 1763; died Dec. 20, 1820; married Margaret Hanna, born Mar. 20,

OTHER DOAK LINES 61

1838 and died 1909 at Lebanon, Tennessee; he married 1762—died 1835.

Their daughter:
III. Mary Campbell Doak, born June 9, 1787; died Nov. 21, 1828; married Sept. 10, 1807, John Billingsley, who was b. Mar. 7, 1786; died Sept. 12, 1844.

Their daughter:
IV. Louise Jane Billingsley, born Jan. 23, 1812; died Nov. 4, 1867; married Nov. 30, 1837, William Blackburn, who was born Dec. 4, 1808; died Jan. 1, 1870.

Their son:
V. Henry Mitchell Blackburn, born Jan. 5, 1846; died Jan. 21, 1923; married Martha Amanda Denpree, Dec. 14, 1869; she was born Jan. 23, 1849; died June 19, 1884.

They had two sons:
VI. (1) James William Blackburn, D.D.S., born Feb. 23, 1875; married Oct. 30, 1907, Ida Greer (b. Oct. 10, 1875). They have two sons: Henry Lee Blackburn, born June 19, 1808; and James William Blackburn, Jr., born Nov. 21, 1814. Dr. James William Blackburn is a prominent dentist in Bowling Green, Kentucky.

(2) John Henry Blackburn, M.D., born Aug. 7, 1876; married May 25, 1904, Bess Trousdale Hatcher, who was born May 5, 1881; they have two sons: Henry Hatcher Blackburn, b. Feb. 8, 1907, and John Denpree Blackburn, b. Sept. 29, 1912. Dr. John Henry Blackburn is a prominent physician of Bowling Green, Kentucky.

CHAPTER IV

SKETCH OF REVEREND SAMUEL DOAK, D.D.

Samuel Doak was a son of Samuel and Jane Mitchell Doak, (married on the voyage over), who emigrated from the North of Ireland and settled first in Chester county, Pennsylvania, but soon thereafter, removed to Augusta County, Virginia, within the bounds of the New Providence Church. They were members of the Presbyterian Church at the time of their marriage and belonged to that division of it that was known as the "Old Side."

It was in August 1749, after their settlement in Virginia that their son, Samuel was born. His father was a farmer and the son's early life was hampered by poverty; although with an unquenchable thirst for knowledge he struggled manfully for an education.

He made a profession of religion when about sixteen years of age and began the study of Lat:n under a Mr. Alexander—probably Archibald, grandfather of the famous Rev. Archibald Alexander, D.D., who was at that time teaching school in the neighborhood.

This school afterwards passed into other hands, and was removed to another place, and subsequently it underwent other changes still, until it finally grew into the institution which was known as Washington College; it is now Washington and Lee University, at Lexington, Virginia.

So great was the desire of Samuel Doak for an education that he proposed to relinquish his share of the patrimonial inheritance to his brothers in order that this education might be obtained. Sold his birthright for an education! His father for a time dissuaded him from the attempt, but observing that it threw him into a discontented and melancholy mood, he determined to gratify his wishes. Young Samuel's funds were low so he "clubbed" with another boy similarly situated; he erected a hut near the school-house, lodged and boarded himself, and became at length assistant teacher, thus acquiring the means of defraying the expenses of his college course. After the completion of his grammar school course he went to West Nottingham Academy at Colora, Maryland, a school founded by Dr. Samuel Finley for young men desiring to enter the ministry.

In 1773, at the age of 24, Samuel Doak entered the College of New Jersey—now Princeton University; being two years advanced in his studies, he was thus ready in 1775 to be admitted to the degree of Bachelor of Arts, during Dr. John Witherspoon's presidency.

After graduating from Princeton, he was, for a short time, an assistant teacher in the school of Rev. Robert Smith, of Pequea, Pennsylvania, and commenced the study of theology under his direction.

On his return to Virginia, he was married to Esther Montgomery, October 31, 1775, she was a daughter of John Montgomery and Esther Houston Montgomery, and a sister of the Reverend John Montgomery, whose family had recently moved from Penn., and were also members of New Providence Church and Community. Shortly after this he accepted the office of Tutor in the new College of Hampden-Sidney, which had been established by the Reverend Samuel Stanhope Smith. Here he remained about two years pursuing the study of theology under the Reverend John Blair Smith, president of the College—he afterwards continued his studies for some time under the Reverend William Graham, of Timber Ridge.

He was licensed to preach the Gospel by the Presbytery of Hanover, on the 31st., day of October, 1777. Having preached for some time in Washington College (now Washington and Lee University, Virginia), he removed to the Holston Settlement, in what was then a part of

North Carolina, but now Sullivan County, Tennessee.

His sister, Elizabeth Thankful Doak, had married Maj. William Hall (of Rev. War) and was living in the Watauga Settlement (now Elizabethton, Tenn.), and it is thought his visit to her prompted his move from Sullivan County. After residing in the Holston Settlement a year or two, he removed in the hope of finding a more promising field of usefulness, to the settlement of Little Limestone, in Washington County, Tennessee, and there purchased a farm on which he built a log house for educational purposes. Historians give a bit of color to this picture by saying: "While in search of a more promising field of usefulness, early in 1780, he met some settlers in the neighborhood of Salem, Tenn., who crowded about him and requested a sermon. Using his horse as a pulpit, he delivered so pleasing and helpful a discourse that they forthwith importuned him to remain among them. Here he remained and purchased a farm on which he built a log house for purposes of education, and a small Church edifice, and immediately gathered the pioneer families under his ministry and their children under his tuition—forming the "Salem Congregation". The literary institution, which he here established was the FIRST that was ever established in the great Valley of the Mississippi—so says Ramsey, the historian.

In 1783 he obtained a charter from the Legislature of North Carolina (which then embraced that part of Tennessee), and again in 1785, he obtained another charter from the Legislature of the State of Franklin (which State existed only two years), in session at Jonesborough (now Jonesboro, Tenn.), on both occasions giving it the name —"Martin Academy", in honor of Governor Alexander Martin, of North Carolina.

Although there remained no record of his work in the school during the first twelve years of its existence, yet, many young men educated by him became useful and eminent—one of them—Dr. J. G. M. Ramsey, in his "Annals of Tennessee", says that it was not only the "first literary institution ever established in the Mississippi

Valley, West of the Alleghenies", but also "for many years the ONLY and for still more, the principal seat of learning in the Western Country". It is not claimed that Samuel Doak was the FIRST Presbyterian Minister on Tennessee soil, but it IS claimed that he was the first to take up his RESIDENCE and to organize a church and school in Tennessee.

In 1772, a few years after the erection of Bean's Cabin, one, perhaps two, churches had been established by the Wolf's Hill or Abingdon (Va.) settlement; the pastor was the Reverend Charles Cummings, of the Abingdon Presbytery, which was formed in 1785 in Augusta County, Virginia, and in 1788 was united to the Synod of the Carolinas.

Dr. Samuel Evans Massengale, of Bristol, Tennessee, in his recent book—"The Massengills, Massengales, and Variants, 1492-1931," and published by the King Printing Company, of Bristol, has a fac simile of an old paper which belonged to Henry Massengill, Sr., and is dated: "Watauga District this 1st day of June 1779," in which is made the statement that—"In April 1777 Rev. Charles Cummings a Presbyterian Minister from Wolf's Hill Settlement came to Watauga and preached three days".

While this may have been Rev. Charles Cummings' first time on Tennessee soil to preach to an assembled congregation, it is a historical fact that he and Rev. Joseph Rhea were Chaplains in the Expedition of Col. William Christian against the Cherokee Indians in 1776, and are the FIRST to have preached at least to the soldiers.

In 1788 the Presbytery of Abingdon formed in Augusta 1785, was united to the Synod of the Carolinas. Here we see the first ORGANIZED introduction of Presbyterianism into Tennessee, for the Abingdon Presbytery lay almost entirely in this State. It was first upon the ground and its ministers were leading figures in the State—they were men of strong character—during these times when the minds of men had not yet been turned to spiritual affairs.

SKETCH OF REVEREND SAMUEL DOAK, D.D.   67

While the Presbyterians were, probably, the first to have established places of worship in Tennessee, it is most likely that the first ministers to PREACH on Tennessee soil were of the Episcopal faith, or one of the established Church of England. When Col. William Byrd began his survey at Currytuck, in 1773, there went along as Chaplain, Rev. Peter Fountaine, an Episcopalian. In 1759-60 when Byrd was sent out to relieve Fort Loudon, he left the Company at Stalnakers', the rest, however, went as far as Long Island, and no doubt the Chaplain went there too.

In Oliver Taylor's "Historic Sullivan" he states that: "The first church to be established on Tennessee soil was called Taylor's Meeting House, and was located in Sullivan County, near Gunnings'—about four miles west of Blountville". To corroborate this statement, Mr. Taylor publishes a letter from a Mr. John S. Jennings who said that his father settled four miles west of Blountville in 1776 and that not only his parents, but grandparents, were members of this church known as Taylor's Meeting House.

Besides this letter Mr. Taylor also published some court records, among them is one dated Jan. 1777 in which road surveys were ordered—"from Steel's Creek to the Meeting House" and "from the Meeting House to Fort Patrick Henry". This antedates, by three months, the coming of Rev. Charles Cummings to the Massengill Settlement in April 1777.

Mr. Taylor states further that Samuel Doak owned a tract of 300 acres of land near there and was associated in the establishing of churches in the community. Upper Concord was formed in 1780 and New Bethel in 1782. Upper Concord is now known as Weaver's (three miles from Bristol), where many of the first settlers are buried. New Bethel has an old grave-yard (so called then) where lie buried ancestors of some of the best families of Sullivan County. The remains of William and Isaac McKinley, relatives of President McKinley lie there.

This bit of reminiscence gives us a general idea of

the country and location of Rev. Samuel Doak's first labors.

Martin Academy which he organized in 1780 and was incorporated in 1785, became Washington College in 1795. The charter was granted by an act of the Legislature of the "Territory of the United States of America, South of the River Ohio", dated July 8, 1795. (For further sketch of the school see Chapter V.)

In 1798 while attending a meeting of the General Assembly at Philadelphia, Penn., Samuel Doak received a donation of classical books for his infant institution, which he transported 500 miles across the mountains on pack horses, and this constituted the nucleus of the library of the present Washington College. Not content with having organized the first SCHOOL, West of the Alleghenies, he now has the distinction of having formed the FIRST LIBRARY West of the Alleghenies.

In 1818 he resigned the presidency of Washington College, after having served in that capacity for thirty-eight years. Soon thereafter he removed to Greene County, within the bounds of Mt. Bethel, where he opened a private school, which he called Tusculum Academy, and which under his son—Rev. Samuel Witherspoon Doak, D.D., grew into Tusculum College, and was chartered in 1844.

Dr. J. G. M. Ramsey—author of "Annals of Tennessee" —was a pupil of Rev. Samuel Doak and in a letter to Mr. Sprague (author of Sprague's Annals of American Pulpit), gives a characteristic description of him, which states: "Dr. Doak was somewhat above the middle statue, had a large muscular frame, well formed, and in later life a little inclined to corpulency—full chested, wide shoulders, and short neck, indicating a strong tendency to apoplexy, of which he died. His appearance was grave and commanding . . . . . the whole countenance expressed strong intellect, manly good sense, calm dignity and indomitable firmness.

"At the age of sixty-five he commenced his chemical studies and though entirely self-taught, he was soon qualified to teach the science to others. About the same time he commenced the study of Hebrew and very soon was able to teach it; and the class which he graduated from Washington College in 1815 was examined upon that language publicly—before an admiring audience, the first class of that kind that ever occurred in Tennessee.

"He read the ancient works on theology in the language in which they were originally written. As a minister one hardly need say that his praise in all our churches. He may well be considered the first apostle of Presbyterianism in Tennessee. No one has been more successful in training young men for the ministry. His style of preaching was original, bold, pungent, and sometimes pathetic. His delivery was natural and impressive, and well fitted to give effect to the truths which he uttered.

"The portrait of Dr. Doak is preserved in the Library of Washington College. The contour of his face bears a strong resemblance to that of John Knox, and the strong pionts of character in the two men were strikingly similar."

Reverend Samuel Doak was not only a preacher and teacher, but, also a true patriot. The sycamores still thrive about the shoals where the forces gathered to march to Kings' Mountain, against Ferguson—and three trees grew from the stump of the one under which he stood when he made his talk and prayer previous to the setting out of the expedition Sept. 26, 1780.

Col. William Campbell, of Virginia, was commanding 400 men, and Col. Isaac Shelby of Sullivan County with the same number—established their Camp at Sycamore Shoals on the Watauga, Sept. 25th. It was the next day, Sept. 26th, that Rev. Samuel Doak was requested to preach to the soldiers before their departure. He selected for his text—"The Sword of the Lord and Gideon" and preached a most powerful sermon; he dismissed them with a prayer of blessing and the combined forces pressed forward in the direction of Gilbert Town, where the enemy was said to be encamped.

Samuel Doak was a Deputy from Washington County, Tennessee to the Convention that met at Jonesboro, Aug. 23, 1784, and a member of the Constitutional Convention of the proposed State of Franklin. He at that time furnished a clause providing for a University to be established by legislature enactment before 1787—"to be endowed liberally." The degree of Doctor of Divinity was conferred upon him by both Washington and Greeneville Colleges in 1818. Greeneville was organized by Rev. Hezekiah Balch and chartered in 1794, but was absorbed by Tusculum College, Nov. 20, 1868, and for a time was known as Greeneville and Tusculum College, but later changed to Tusculum College. Rev. Charles O. Gray was the president for many years.

It was here at Tusculum (Bethel Church) that Reverend Samuel Doak, D.D., passed the residue of his life in honor and usefulness, and died in his 82nd. year on the 12th, day of December, 1830.

His first wife Esther Houston Montgomery, died on the 3rd, July 1807. He was afterwards married to Mrs. Margaretta (Houston) McEwen, widow of Alexander McEwen and a sister of the Reverend Samuel Houston. She died Sept. 22, 1831. He had five children—two sons and three daughters—all by his first wife.

His influence and usefulness are indescribable. As a teacher he was well qualified, apt to teach, diligent and successful. He won the name "Apostle of Learning and Religion in the West", and was often spoken of as "The Father of Education in Tennessee".

Dr. Doak rests in the Cemetery of Old Salem Church which adjoins the College Campus. The large oak trees that shade his grave in all probability were standing when he preached his first sermon to the hardy pioneers.

"He is dead—yet speaketh,
His influence will never die".

CHAPTER V

WASHINGTON COLLEGE

Washington College was formed from Martin Academy, which was founded by Reverend Samuel Doak in 1780, and was first chartered by North Carolina April 24, 1783; second charter was granted by the "Lost State of Franklin," March 31, 1785; the third, and present charter, from "Territory of the United States, South of River Ohio," July 8, 1795.

The Academy had received 420 acres of land on the Doe River, from Colonel Waightstill Avery, besides numerous contributions of money, and later, Alexander Mathes donated a valuable tract of fifty acres adjoining the property of Mr. Doak, where the college building then stood, and which is the present site of the modern institution.

Reverend Samuel Doak was president from the time of its organization in 1780 until 1818, when he resigned after having served for thirty-eight years.

The first graduates of Martin Academy were, John Whitfield Doak (eldest son of Rev. Samuel) and James Witherspoon, who received their degrees on Aug. 15, 1796. It is stated that long prior to the War Between the States that twenty-two members of Congress of the United States had completed their education at Washington College, under this pioneer in letters and religious training.

The first geography published in the United States did not appear until 1784—four years after Samuel Doak opened the first school in Tennessee. The title of same was: "Geography Made Easy" by Jedidiah Morse.

THE DOAK FAMILY

Reverend John Whitfield Doak was made Vice-President of Washington College in 1806 and commissioned to solicit funds in Georgia and South Carolina, where he obtained $836.65. The next year he visited the North and East and secured $1575.00. With these funds a new frame building was erected in 1808.

When Rev. Samuel Doak resigned the presidency in 1818 he was succeeded by his son, the Reverend Samuel Witherspoon Doak, who continued in office until his death in 1820.

John W. Bovell was president from 1820-1829; Rev. James McLin from 1829-1838; Rev. Samuel Witherspoon Doak from 1838-1840. In 1840 a new college building was erected at a cost of $6000.00; at the same time a dwelling for the president was erected. These buildings were completed in 1842, and the institution under the presidency of Reverend Archibald Alexander Doak (son of Rev. John Whitfield Doak), from 1840-1850, entered upon an era of greater prosperity than it had known for several preceding years.

Reverend E. Thompson Baird was president from 1850-1852, at which time Rev. A. A. Doak was prevailed upon to again accept the presidency, which he did—serving from 1852-1856.

Reverend Samuel Hodge, D.D., pastor of Salem Church, on the College Campus, conducted the school from 1857-1862 (not college grade), and Misses Eva A., and G. Adda Telford, from 1866-1868 (not college grade). The succeeding presidents of Washington College have been: Rev. W. B. Rankin, D.D., 1868-1867; Rev. J. E. Alexander, D.D., 1877-1883; Rev. J. W. C. Willoughby, D.D., 1883-1891; Rev. James T Cooter, D.D., 1891-1923; Rev. Charles O. Gray, D.D., was president of Washington and Tusculum College, which were united from 1908-1913. Dr. Gray was for many years the President of Tusculum College. The thirteenth president was Reverend Hubert S. Lyle, D.D., who served from 1923 until his death in 1931.

Professor John Milton Scott, A.B., L.I., who has been instructor of Latin at Washington College for twenty-eight years, and for several years Secretary of the Board of Trustees, is now directing the affairs of the school pending the selection of a new president. He has the hearty co-operation of Rev. James T. Cooter, D.D., who has given forty-three years of earnest hard work for Washington College as President, President Emeritus and Field Representative.

The College is now co-educational and doing a most wonderful work for the young people of this mountain section of East Tennessee. Through their department of SMITH-HUGHES AGRICULTURE the boys are trained to be practical farmers—real THINKING farmers who will endeavor not only to raise bumper crops, but marketable products. They receive considerable training in their shop work and are taught to repair anything in the line of machinery that is used on the farm.

This program of work encourages them to be wide-awake as to the possibilities of by-products from the farm kitchen, the dairy, the dairy barn, etc. They are keenly interested in substitutes for lumber and leather which some of our leading industrialists are experimenting with, the production of which will add to the farmers' income.

The girls, in their splendidly equipped home economics department, have an equally practical and progressive program.

Washington College is a "self-help" school. No student is admitted who is financially able to pay his own way through school. Each student works three hours each day and all day on Monday. This service and one hundred dollars, makes it possible for a student to go to school at this institution for an entire year, board, room and tuition included.

Many church organizations, as well as individuals, avail themselves of the privilege to assist worthy girls and boys of this mountain section.

The atmosphere of Washington College is very refreshing—clean, wholesome, honest, straightforward, constructive and vitally Christian.

In May, 1931, during their Commencement week, the school observed its 151st anniversary, with a beautiful historic pageant, depicting the early life and work of the Reverend Samuel Doak, D.D.

Chapter VI

MISCELLANEOUS RECORDS

DOAK—BRECKENRIDGE.
(From *Virginia Soldiers of 1776*, by Louis A. Burgess, Vol. II, pages 586-733.)

p. 586.

Alexander Breckenridge served in the Virginia line. He was a son of George Breckenridge (married 1742 ANN DOAK), who was a son of Alexander Breckenridge and Jane Preston.

Captain Alexander Breckenridge married 1767, Magdalen Gamble; their son, John, married first, Ann Wier Brooks, daughter of Abigail Brooks; their daughter, Ann E., married Lafayette Ardery in 1852 and had William Porter Ardery, who in 1880 married Ella Adair. William Porter and Ella Adair Ardery were the parents of William Breckenridge Ardery, etc.

p. 732.

THE BRECKENRIDGE FAMILY.
From *Times Dispatch*.

Alexander Breckenridge came to America in 1728, remained some years in Pennsylvania and was living in Augusta county, Virginia, in 1738.

On Feb. 21, 1738, Alexander, George, James, Robert and Adam Breckenridge entered warrants for 100 acres of land, each with Benjamin Borden.

In 1740 Alexander Breckenridge proved in Orange county the importation of himself and family. The names of three of the children are illegible. It is probable that one of them is Adam. In 1751 there is a suit stating that Adam Breckenridge "had gone to North Carolina."

On March 16, 1758, the will of Adam Breckenridge is proved.

May 24, 1744, the widow of Alexander Breckenridge (Jane Preston) relinquished administration of his estate to her eldest son, George Breckenridge. Alexander and Jane Preston Breckenridge had children:

I. George Breckenridge, married ANN DOAK; she died Mar. 1748; he died in Wythe county, Virginia, 1790; their son, CAPTAIN ALEXANDER BRECKENRIDGE, married 1767, Magdalen Gamble. More later.

II. Col. Robert Breckenridge (his war records not copied), married first, Mary Poague, daughter of Robert Poague of Augusta county; he married second, Lettie Preston, daughter of John Preston; he died in Botetourt county, Virginia, 1772. (Children will be given later).

III. Lettice Breckenridge, married Sept., 1749, Elijah McClanahan.

IV. James Breckenridge and two other sons.

I. GEORGE and ANN DOAK BRECKENRIDGE, had the following children:

1. Captain Alexander Breckenridge, married 1767 Magdalen Gamble; he died in Bourbon, Kentucky, 1813.

2. Robert, born 1743; died in Bath county, Kentucky, 1814; married MARY DOAK (daughter of the Emigrant Robert Doak, who married a Breckenridge).

3. John Breckenridge, married Elizabeth Willoughby; died in Bourbon county, Kentucky.

4. Elizabeth Breckenridge, married Jesse Evans.

5. Letitia Breckenridge, married a Lindsey.

6. Sarah Breckenridge, married a Findley.

7. Jane Breckenridge, married an Alcorn.

II. COL. ROBERT and MARY POAGUE BRECKENRIDGE, had the following children:

1. Lieut. Robert (war records not copied), died Sept. 11, 1833. D. Breckenridge, M. C. from Kentucky.

Children of Col. Robert Breckenridge and his second wife, Lettice Preston Breckenridge, were:

2. Capt. Alexander (war records not copied), removed to Kentucky and married Jane, widow of Col. John Floyd, and daughter of Col. John Buchanan. One of their sons was James

3. William Breckenridge, of Augusta county, and Lexington, Kentucky, married a Miss Gilliam.

4. John Breckenridge, born Dec. 2, 1760; died Dec. 14, 1806. He was a member of the House of Delegates of Virginia; removed in 1793 to Kentucky where he occupied prominent offices and was Attorney-General of the United States from 1805 until his death. He married Feb. 22, 1789, Mary Hopkins, daughter of Col. Joseph Cabell of Buckingham county; they had issue: (1) Letitia, married first, Alfred W. Grayson, son of U. S. Senator William Grayson; she married second Gen. Peter H. Porter of New York, who was Secretary of War, U. S., from 1828-29. (2) Joseph Cabell Breckenridge; (3) Rev. John Breckenridge; (4) Rev. Robert Breckenridge; (5) Rev. William L. Breckenridge.

5. James Breckenridge, served in the Revolution in Col. Preston's Regt., under Gen. Greene; he was born Mar. 7, 1763, and resided at "Grove Hill," Botetourt county, Virginia; died May 13, 1833; married Jan. 1, 1791, Ann Selden, a daughter of Cary Selden, of Elizabeth City, county. Among his descendants were: Capt. James Breckenridge, a cavalry officer in the Confederate line (see Va. Mag. of Hist., Vol. 27, and Selden's Va. and Allied Families).

Another son of James and Ann Selden Breckenridge, was John, who married Miss Heiskell; their daughter, Susan, married Anthony Diggs Wren, and died Apr. 22, 1885, aged 62. Anthony D. Wren died Sept. 20, 1886, aged 68; their son, John Breckenridge Wren, born 1848, married Mar. 1, 1876, Ella Margaret Campbell, born 1858, and a daughter of Anthony Campbell and Margaret Nickell; their daughter, Alma Bell Wren, married Lorenzo Sibert Evans, and had—Marie Anne (married Edward Lapham Steele), and Lorenzo Sibert Evans, Jr.

TATE—DOAK.
(From *Boone Family History*, by Dr. R. N. Mayfield.)

John Tate, who migrated from Pennsylvania to Virginia in 1743, married MARY DOAK and was one of the founders of Augusta county, Virginia. He owned a farm and mill. He died in 1801. Their known children were:

1. James Tate, who came from Pennsylvania with his parents and later lived near Greeneville, Virginia. He was killed at Guilford, Virginia.

2. Col. John Tate (later known as "senior"), was born 1743, died 1828; married Mary Bracken. He moved with his family in 1772 to that section of Virginia that was later formed into what is now Russell county, etc., etc.

3. William Tate.
4. Robert Tate.
5. Thomas Tate.
6. A daughter—who married Francis Beaty.

Editor's Note: The above information would indicate that there was still another Doak sister—Emigrant Mary Doak, who married the above John Tate. However, it is possible that this Mary belongs to another Doak family, but if any reader has definite information on this line the author of this book will appreciate a letter from same.

ROBERT AND WILLIAM DOAK.

(From *Annals of Tazewell County, Virginia*, by J. N. Harman.) Page 23.

In 1768 the settlers were beginning to petition the County Court of Augusta to assume jurisdiction over the territory which had been disputed land and by treaties reorganized as belonging to the Indians.

In that year the inhabitants of Reed creek of Holston, filed their petition, requesting they be permitted to settle and cultivate land, etc., and "that there may be alterations and amendments on the old road leading from Captain Ingles' Ferry to James Davis, on the head of the Holston River, and appoint such surveyors as you in your wisdom shall think fit, and your petitioners as is duty bound will pray."

SIGNERS:

Joseph Black,	Robert Doack,
James Holice,	William Doack,
John Montgomery,	George Breckenridge,
Robert Montgomery,	Alexander Breckenridge,
James Montgomery,	Robert Breckenridge,

and many others.

John Campbell, on his way to the Holston in 1768, overtook a number of persons who informed him they were coming to settle on a tract of land owned by Dr. Thomas Walker, known as the WOLF HILL TRACT (now Abingdon, Va.)

In 1768 ROBERT DOACK sowed turnips on Reed Creek, but made no settlement. ROBERT DOACK was Dr. Thomas Walker's agent for the Wolf Hill Tract, and Thomas Armstrong was one of the earliest settlers.

In the year 1771, John Montgomery went to Big Moccasin Creek with his father Alexander Montgomery.

NOTES ON THE DOAK FAMILY
From Chaulkley's Abstracts of Augusta County Records.

"Samuel Doak, emigrant, married on voyage, Jane Mitchell." (From History of Rockbridge County, Virginia.)
Chaulkley's. Vol. III, p. 123.

WILL OF SAMUEL DOAK: Will book No. 4, p. 497; Nov. 5, 1771; to wife, Jane, and her three daughters, Elinor, Mary and Isbel; to son, John; to oldest son, David, plantation David now lives on as laid out by Robert Doak; to son, Samuel, plantation at headwaters of Rockfish in Amherst; to son, John; to son, Robert; to daughters, Jane and Elizabeth.

Executors, wife, Jane, son, David, and son-in-law, William Brown, and brother-in-law, John Finley. Proved May 19, 1772. Vol. II, p. 8.

In 1775 Samuel Doak, from a military warrant under the King of Great Britain's proclamation, had a survey made including a settlement on waters of Reed Creek (then in Fincastle, now —1802—in Wythe county). Samuel Doak went to live in North Carolina (now Tennessee) about 1789 and has not returned.

(Editor's Note: This is too late for the Rev. Samuel unless there is an error in that date, as the Rev. Samuel went to Tennessee (then North Carolina) about 1780 or earlier.

Betsey Wilson Doak, daughter of John Doak. Vol. III, p. 228.

David Doage, military claim for provisions, Apr. 15, 1765. Vol. I, p. 120.

David Doak, hemp certificate, Mar. 15, 1768. Vol. I, p. 144.

David Doage, marriage license for—no woman's name, Oct. 30, 1762. Vol. II, p. 276.

David Doak and wife, Janett, give consent to marriage of Jennie Doak to James Berry, Jan. 6, 1787. Robert Doak and John Doak, witnesses. Vol. II, p. 301.

David Doak's daughter, Elizabeth, licensed to marry John Larew, Mar. 11, 1799. Samuel Doak is surety. Samuel is brother to Elizabeth. Vol. II, p. 327.

Emigrant David Doak, Constable—1756—delinquent—1756. Vol. II, p. 318.

Emigrant David Doak, land surveyed for, Mar. 26, 1748.
David Doak, land surveyed for, 1756, Vol. II, p. 444.
David Doak, land surveyed for, 1766, Vol. II, p. 456.

The Doak Family

David Doak, purchased 100 acres in Beverley Manor 1755, for 8 pounds. Vol. III, p. 337.

David Doak, purchased 300 acres in Beverley Manor, from George and Robert Breckenridge, Feb. 10, 1745-46. Paid 42 pounds Virginia money. Vol. III, p. 252.

David Doak, mentioned in will of Samuel Doak as eldest son, given plantation he now lives on, Nov. 5, 1771. Vol. III, p. 123.

David Doak, mentioned in will of his father, John Doak, who also mentions a brother, David, Mar. 21, 1804. Vol. III, p. 228.

David Doak's will: June 26, 1799; wife, Jennet; to sons, Samuel and David; to daus., Jenny Berry, Rosannah Doak, Betsey, and to five daughters, namely: Aggy, Fanny, Dorcas, Polly, Elly; to son, Hugh. Executors, wife, Jennet, sons, Samuel and David; guardian, James Berry; witnesses, Thomas Mitchell, James and Samuel Meteer; proved June 28, 1806; Jennet refused to act; the others qualified. Vol. III, p. 222.

David Doak and wife, Mary, sell 400 acres to John Alexander, of York county, Pennsylvania, for 310 pounds, May 16, 1769. Vol. III, p. 487.

David Doak, witness when John Alexander gives mortgage on above 400 acres, "sold him by David Doak where on David Doak formerly lived," Nov. 18, 1771. Vol. III, p. 514.

Dorcas Doak, daughter of John Doak, mentioned in his will, 1804. Vol. III, p. 240.

Dorcas Doak, daughter of David Doak, mentioned in his will, June 26, 1799. Vol. III, p. 222.

Dorcas Doak, witness to James Mateer's will—perhaps the wife of Robert Doak, who is also a witness, Oct. 25, 1812. Vol. III, p. 240.

Elizabeth Doak, daughter of Robert Doak, marriage license to John Lilley, April 10, 1797, by Rev. Archibald Scott. The same paragraph also mentions her as daughter of JOHN Doak. Vol. II, p. 327-356.

Elizabeth Doak, daughter of David Doak, licensed to marry John Larew, Mar. 11, 1799. Vol. II, p. 333.

Isabella Doak, marriage license to John Milliken, Sept. 27, 1786, by Rev. Archibald Scott. Vol. II, p. 347.

James Doak, cash paid for teaching of Blackwood, Mar., 1795. In settlement of Blackwood estate. Vol. I, p. 274.

John Doak, William Casteel is bound to John Doak, Apr. 19, 1786. Vol. I, p. 245.

Miscellaneous Records

John Doak, qualified as Major of 2nd Battalion, 32nd Regt., 7th Brigade, Aug. 21, 1798. Vol. I, p. 289.

John Doak mentioned as brother of Samuel Doak, Vol. I, p. 204.

John Doak, witness to marriage license of Jennie Doak and James Berry, Jan. 6, 1787. Vol. II, p. 301.

John Doak has lived on land since death of his father, Samuel Doak, who lived on it upwards of 60 years, Aug. 26, 1806. Vol. II, p. 32.

John Doak says he is the father of Elizabeth Doak, in marriage license to John Lilley, Apr. 10, 1798. Vol. II, p. 327.

John Doak a member of Capt. John Christians' company, 1742. Vol. II, p. 509.

John Doak's will: Proved June 23, 1806. dated Mar. 21, 1804; to son, John; to sons Samuel and Thomas Mitchell Doak; to dau., Julia; to dau., Nancy; dau., Rosannah; dau., Betsey Wilson Doak; son, Washington; son, David; Executors, brothers, Robert, Samuel, Sr., and David. Vol. III, p. 228.

John Doage, farmer, to Richard Burton, farmer, 400 acres on west side of Blue Ridge, patented to John, Jan. 12, 1746; Nov. 19, 1747. Vol. III, p. 266.

Nancy Doak, witness to will of James Mateer, Oct. 25, 1812. Vol. III, p. 240.

Robert Doage—recommended for Justice, June 22, 1769. Vol. I, p. 157.

Robert Doage—recommended for Captain, Apr. 18, 1787. Vol. I, p. 249.

Robert Doage—for land—see Vol. I, p. 497-498.

Robert Doak, recommended as Captain, Mar. 22, 1793. Vol. I, p. 272.

Robert Doak, qualified as Captain, Vol. I, p. 272-274.

Robert Doak, purchased land—120 acres—on branch of Looney's Creek, 1769. Vol. III, p. 435.

Robert Doak, agent for Dr. Thomas Walker, land surveyor, 1769. Vol. II, p. 123.

Robert Doak elected overseer of the poor, Mar. 29, 1791. Vol. III, p. 194.

Robert Doack, marriage license, Augusta Co., Va., name of wife not given, Mar. 28, 1774.

Robert Doak, buys on South River, called Buffer Hill (Buffalo Hill), Mar. 16, 1779. Vol. III, p. 557.

The Doak Family

Robert Doak, one of men representing Bethel Meeting House who purchased land from John Waddell and others, Apr. 16, 1782. Vol. III, p. 565.

Robert Doak, mentioned as brother and executor of will of John Doak, Mar. 21, 1804. Vol. III, p. 228.

Robert Doak, witness to will of Thomas Mitchell, senior, Aug. 6, 1805. Vol. III, p. 229.

Samuel Doak. The will of Samuel Doak, the emigrant, has been given.

Samuel Doak—Peter Kinder vs. Samuel Doak—bill 16th, June, 1802. In 1770 Andrew Little made a settlement on Reed Creek, then in Fincastle, now Wythe Co., and a short time afterwards transferred it to John Riley, who sold to orator. In 1775 Samuel Doak from a military warrant under the King of Great Britain's proclamation, had a survey made including above settlement. The warrant to Samuel was dated 1773 and under the proclamation of 1763. Samuel Doak went to live in North Carolina (now Tennessee) about 1789 and has never returned.

The answer to this states: In 1768 Robert Doak, for and on behalf of Samuel Doak, sowed some turnips on the land, but made no settlement. In 1770 Jacob Young made an improvement on the same tract but removed to Holston and conveyed his claim to Samuel Doak. In 1771 Samuel Doak built a cabin and afterwards Andrew Little built a cabin but never lived in it.

George Boyd of Stuart county, Tennessee, deposes, 3rd, December, 1804.

Samuel Doak, survey made for, Mar. 26, 1748. Vol. II, p. 434-456.

Samuel Doak, executor of will of John Greer, Sept. 15, 1750. Vol. III, p. 18.

Samuel Doak and John Mitchell are guardians of orphans of John Greer, Nov. 22, 1752. Vol. I, p. 66; also Vol. III, p. 26.

Samuel Doak, member of Capt. John Christian's Company, 1742, Vol. II, p. 32—also p. 509.

Samuel Doak in Capt. James Mitchell's Company of processioners, 1755. Vol. II, p. 442.

Samuel Doak, mentioned as Constable and delinquent in taxes, 1755. Vol. II, p. 417.

Samuel Doak mentioned as brother of Elizabeth, who married John Larew, 1799, and son of David Doak.

William Doack signed petition concerning road from Capt. Ingles' Ferry to head of Holston.

William Doack, witness, May 16, 1769, when David Doak, emigrant, and Mary sell land. Vol. III, p. 487.

William Doack, was Justice or Judge in a case, June 16, 1769. Vol. III, p. 556.

NOTES FROM THE HISTORY OF ROCKBRIDGE COUNTY, VIRGINIA.

Samuel Doak, immigrant married on voyage, Jane Mitchell.

Samuel Doak, brother of John, was administrator to David Steele, 1747.

Robert Doak, the immigrant, married ——— Breckenridge, sister of Robert Breckenridge.

James Doak, son of Robert the Emigrant, and ——— Breckenridge, married Jane Dunn. (For further Breckenridge data—see elsewhere).

John W. Doak, born 1770, married Jane McClure.

Ann Doak, born 1784, married Hugh McGuffey, page 482.

FROM SUMMERS' *ANNALS OF SOUTHWEST VIRGINIA*.

Robert Doach, qualified as Magistrate and took his seat, Botetourt Co., Feb. 14, 1770. Page 109.

Robert Doach, Fall of 1772—member of House of Burgesses, was present Jan. 5, 1773, at the first County Court for Fincastle held at Lead Mines on New River. (Editor's Note—this is now Wythe Co., Va.) Page 130.

Robert Doach—surveyor of land and mentioned as "Captain Robert Doach." Pages 269-270-622.

David Doack—Montgomery Co., Va., Abstract of Will: His estate to his wife, Mary, and his children, 9 sons and 4 daughters; children mentioned, David, John, Nathaniel, and Samuel. Witnesses, William Davis, John Wilson, Henry Newman. Probated Oct. 2, 1787, and proven by Henry Newman.

David Doak, Aug. 1, 1768, bought for 300 pounds, 1020 acres at Black Buffalo Lick on the waters of Wood River (now New River), from John McFarlin and his wife, Mary. Page 531.

David Doak, Jr., recommended as 2nd Lieut. in Ward's Company. Page 758.

David Doak, Jr., First Lieut. in Capt. John Ward's Company of Militia, Apr. 2, 1782. Montgomery Co., Va. Page 762.

David Doak, among those recommended to the Governor as officers for County Militia was—David Doak, Wythe Co., Va., May 26, 1790.

Samuel Doak took oath for Deputy, Montgomery Co., Va., Jun. 5, 1779. Page 699.

Samuel Doak, Montgomery Co., Va., recommended as Ensign, in Militia of the county. Sept. 8, 1779. Page 725.

Samuel Doak, Cavalry—from neighborhood of Tinkling Spring, 1812. (Hist. of Aug. Co., Va., by Peyton).

James Doak (was in Fincastle Co.) now takes oath in Montgomery Co.—Sheriff Feb. 2, 1779. Page 701.

James Doak, recommended 2nd Lieut. in Company of William Ward. Page 754.

DOAK MARRIAGES.

David Doak, to Rachel Gibb, Apr. 8, 1787, Montgomery Co., Va., by Rev. Richard Whitt. Page 903.

The following are from Chalkley's Augusta County Records:

Isabella Doak, to John Milliken, Sept. 27, 1786.

Jennie Doak (daughter of David and Jannet Doak), to James Berry, Mar. 10, 1787.

Elizabeth Doak (daughter of Robert), to John Lilly, Apr. 10, 1797.

Elizabeth Doak (daughter of David) to John Larew, Mar. 11, 1799.

Chapter VII

DOAK WILLS

LAST WILL AND TESTAMENT OF REVEREND SAMUEL DOAK.
(Will book I, page 90. Probated in the County Court of Greene County, Tennessee, Jan. 25, 1831.)

I, Samuel Doak of Greene County (lately of Washington), Tennessee, being in perfect health and sound state of mind do make and ordain this my last will and testament, inprimis:

I give and bequeath to my son Johney Whitfield Doak the whole of the tract of land on which I lately lived in Washington County, and all its appurtenances to be his estate forever after my death; also whatever else I have given him shall be his.

I will and bequeath to my son Samuel Witherspoon Doak, all my movable property of every description after all just debts against it are paid, as negroes, &c, with the exception below.

Item—I will and bequeath & confirm to my daughters Julia, Lorinda, Jane Rowe, Nancy and Polly Montgomery, the right and title to all the property of every description which I give to them, i.e., to each of them the portion of property which I gave to her at her marriage or departure from my house.

I will and bequeath to my beloved wife Margaretta, one good bed with its appurtenances, one gray mare now known in the family by the name of her mare and the sum of seventy-two dollars with whatever interest may arise from that sum from this time, to be at her sole disposal living or dying; yet I would barely advise her to leave whatever may remain when she shall cease to have a call for them or at her death to whichever of my sons may have the charge of her maintenance. Also that her maintenance may be sure, full and decent during natural and single life I do secure it on the absolute condition of my son Johney's getting the undivided possession of the land above mentioned as left to him. I also will that if she choose to live with my son Johney she have the exclusive right to possess that part of the house which I lately occupied in Washington County, which has been known in the family by the name of my room; also if she choose to live with my son Samuel I will that she derive her maintenance as above described out of the property which I left to him so that her maintenance above described is an absolute condition of his undivided possession of the same.

ITEM—I also will and bequeath to my step-son Alexander McEwen all the expenses I have been at in boarding, clothing, & educating him, also one saddle and bridle and a sorrel mare, all of which I have given him.

Finally—I appoint and ordain my two sons Johney W. & Samuel W. Doak & David Rice Executors, & Margaretta Doak Executrix of this my last will and testament, which is published, pronounced and declared on this the 30th day of December in the year of our Lord one thousand eight hundred and eighteen and signed by me in the presence of—

Signed, SAM'L DOAK.

Test:
JAMES GALBREATH,
SAMUEL ROBINSON,
JAMES PATTERSON,
JAMES S. JOHNSON.

ABSTRACTED WILL OF JOHN WHITFIELD DOAK.
(From records of Washington County, Tennessee; Book I, p. 129.)

Will of John W. Doak, of Washington County, Aug. 23, 1820.

Mentions—"wife Jane."

"When youngest child is of age."

Sons: "Samuel Harvey, and John Newton Doak"—plantation on the waters of Little Limestone, where I now live.

Two other sons: Archibald Alexander and James Witherspoon Doak.

"My four daughters: Sophia Doak, Esther Montgomery Doak, Eliza Smith Doak, and Jane Doak, the proceeds from the sale of my lands in Kentucky.

William Mitchell, John Nelson, Jr., and Eleaza L. Mathes, Executors.

Signed, JOHN W. DOAK.

Testators:
JOHN McLESTER,
JOHN PATTEN,
GEORGE BELL.

WILL OF JOHN NEWTON DOAK—Abstract.
(From records of Cannon County, Tennessee.)

Wife—Emily T. Doake, land beginning at Thomas Doke's and Joseph Bailey's line; dau. Martha E. Doak; dau. Annie F. Bailey; son Thomas J. Doak; son R. D. Doak; son John N. Doak; dau. Thankful Preston; dau. Mary H. Davis.

Son Thomas J. Doak, and son-in-law Hugh L. Preston, executors, June 3, 1881.

Signed, JOHN N. DOAK.

Teste:
C. E. CUBLES,
G. O. STROUD.
Proven—September 1881.

SAMUEL W. DOAK
AND
M. S. DOAK

AGREEMENT: April 21, 1858.
ACKNOWLEDGED: January 11, 1862, before E. W. Headrick, Clerk.
RECORDED: January 11, 1862, in Deed Book No. 32, page 496.
COVENANTS: None.

Know all men by these presents, that Samuel W. Doak and Matthew S. Doak both of Greene County and State of Tennessee have thrown together all they possess or own of property such as lands, houses, animals, farming instruments household and kitchen furniture, books, &c, &c, so that they are hereafter to have one common ownership, right and interest in all things they now have or hereafter shall have & all the outstanding debts due to either party, and all the debts which either party owes with the understanding, namely, that in case the decision of a suit now in the Court of Chancery with Samuel Snapp shall settle the value of Georgia St. Bonds, got of him in the year 1842, at fifty cents a dollar, then Mary J. Cox and Lourinda C. Ramsey, besides an outfit such as Eliza F. R. Gibson and Julia M. Anderson received on leaving the family in a horse, saddle, bridle, cow & households and kitchen furniture &c, receive each one hundred dollars, also S. S. M. Doak; J. W. K. Doak & Elizabeth F. R. Gibson receive fifty dollars; Alexander M. Doak one hundred dollars & Robert E. & William S. Doak each two hundred dollars & Julia M. Anderson one hundred dollars, also that the interest on five hundred dollars be exclusively allowed to the said Sam'l W. Doak & his wife Sarah K. Doak or either of them who may survive the other as long as he or she may live to be used as he or she may please & when both are dead the principal is to belong to Matthew S. Doak.

Moreover it is agreed by the parties that whichsoever may survive the other shall have the right to convey by his last Will & testament or otherwise after the above sums & all the debts are paid, all the property &c remaining among the heirs only of the said Matthew S. Doak provided he shall have heirs of his own body. But in case he shall die leaving no heirs of his own body his wife Margaret is to have an estate equal to that which any of his sisters shall have received & the balance then is to be conveyed or distributed equally to the brothers and sisters of the said Matthew S. Doak. Moreover it is clearly understood that the parties are living together & that their wives are to have a full decent and comfortable support while living and decent burial when dead. In testimony whereof we hereunto subscribe our names and affix our seals in presence of—

A. D. HALE,
JESSE WALLIN,
JOHN V. DOAK. April 21, 1858.

S. W. DOAK,
M. S. DOAK.

Know all men by these presents, that since the suit in Chancery Court referred to in an article of agreement signed by us—S. W. Doak and M. S. Doak, on the 21st of April 1858 has been so as to compel the said S. W. Doak to pay John Snapp, Sam'l E. Snapp & Elijah Carson and for costs fourteen hundred and seventy one dollars more than anticipated for one half of the claim against the said S. W. Doak while the other half of said claim had been settled with Eliza D. Doak & husband heirs to that half according to their own request by the payment of five hundred and sixty two dollars and a half interest thereon on the 3rd day of March 1859.

Now we the parties do agree that the article shall be so altered in consequence of said loss of said $1471, as to require the payment to the heirs of the said S. W. Doak as follows, viz. to S. S. M. Doak one dollar, to J. W. K. Doak one dollar, to E. F. R. Gibson one dollar, to A. M. Doak fifty dollars, R. E. Doak seventy-five dollars, Julia M. Anderson twenty five dollars, L. C. Ramsey twenty five dollars, & a horse worth seventy five dollars, W. S. Doak one dollar, & Robert M. Cox only child of M. J. Cox one hundred dollars when called for by himself in boarding, tuition, &c, at Tusculum College after 10 years from this date. In all other respects the said article to remain in full force.

Witness our hands & seals, the 13th day of January, 1862.

S. W. DOAK,
M. S. DOAK.

Chapter VIII

MATHEWS-MATHES

A letter from Miss I. C. VanDeventer, of Kansas City, Mo., gives many interesting details of family history, and it is therefore quoted here in full.

503 Munford Court,
Kansas City, Mo.,
May 30, 1933.

My dear Mrs. French:

I am in receipt of copies of The Lookout and also your letter, and find the Doak data interesting. Hope you have more of the early history in your book, as that is what I am interested in. Had hoped that you would have the date of marriage of Samuel Doak and Jane Mitchell, as they were married on the voyage that would have given us the date of their coming. Note that you place the date of their coming to America at about 1740. Our data handed down in the family, placed the date about 1720, and it may have been between those dates. I doubt if they came as early as 1720, but possibly before 1740, as Samuel Doak, Jr., is placed as the sixth child, born in 1749, so it is probable that his parents were married prior to 1740. A John Mathews, emigrant from the North of Ireland, is said to have come in 1737, and as his history runs parallel with ours and he settled in the Beverly grant, he may have been a brother to our George. His descendants have been prominent and there is much about them in the reference books. They were prominent in the Revolution and his son, George, was three times Governor of Georgia.

As to the spelling of the name, it was originally Mathews (one "t"). George Mathews, who emigrated with Samuel Doak, Sr., had 12 sons and one daughter. Four of the sons, Alexander, Allen, Jeremiah and George, when they went from Virginia to Tennessee dropped the "w" and spelled the name Mathes—the tradition is, so that their descendants would know each other. So, please use that spelling in your book—it was never spelled with "l".

In part IV of The Lookout article you have Jane Doak, daughter of Rev. John Whitfield Doak, married Ezekiel Mathes. Some one has made a mistake there, as Ezekiel Salmon Mathes married (Nov. 21, 1853) Mary Jane Bovell, daughter of Dr. William Ward Bovell, and great-granddaughter of Samuel Doak, founder of Washington College. So she was a daughter of Eliza Jane Doak, who married Dr. Bovell (and not her sister). This Ezekiel S. Mathes was b. Oct. 31, 1830, d. May 31, 1903, was son of Alexander Mathes III (b. Aug. 29, 1800, d. Feb. 14, 1884); son of Alexander Mathes II, b. Oct. 5, 1775, in Va., d. Feb. 12, 1865, in Tennessee; son of George Mathews, the immigrant. Am sure the above is correct, as my aunt knew them and Ezekiel Mathes was her cousin.

Mary Jane Bovell was a half sister to Annie Adella Bovell (or Annis), who married John Shields Mathes, the younger brother of Ezekiel, and whose daughter, Mrs. Essie M. Turner, lives in Jonesboro, Tenn. John S. Mathes was greatly interested in historical matters and wrote much of Tennessee history. We are indebted to him for preserving data for the beginning of our family history. He had intended to write a history of the Mathes family, but died before accomplishing that purpose. It was said of him that "It seems a pity that one so well qualified as he and who had written so entertainingly of other families, should have left the history of his own unfinished."

In part VII of The Lookout article you have Mary Lou, daughter of John Whitfield Doak (b. 1814) m. William Mathes. I do not have that item, but would like to work it out and find out which William this is (have about nine in the list). I note that this family went to Georgia, and we have a William Mathes, a miller, son of John (b. April 4, 1786); son of Alexander I, who married Susan Mathes, his cousin (daughter of George Leith Mathes) and went to Georgia, and it may have been his son who married Mary Lou Doak. We have no record of his descendants. Have not his date of birth, but his brother, Archibald Alexander Mathes, was born in 1812, so that the son should be about the right age. Have a very good line of Archibald Alexander Mathes' descendants, but William dropped out of sight. Are you in touch with any one who could furnish more information on this?

We have Alexander Calvin Mathes, b. May 5, 1808, who married Miss Doak (first name not known), and have nothing more about them. He was a son of George Leith Mathes (b. Sept. 24, 1779, son of Alexander I) and Phoebe Wear Alexander Calvin's brother Ebenezer E. Mathes, m. Margaret L. Wilson and had a son, Calvin Alexander Mathes (b. 1844), whose daughter, Ethel, married Dr. Fred W. Alexander, President of Stonewall Jackson College, Abingdon, Va. Another daughter, Georgie Bell, married David Alexander, brother of Fred.

I note that John Whitfield Keith Doak married a West. We have some West connection and I have some data on that family. Leonora Ruble was a West descendant, and she married McFarland M. Mathes of Washington College.

I note the name of Jane Rowe Doak. My grandmother was Jane Roe Mathes.

The Mathews and Doak families emigrated from Ireland together, and I have the notation that their home there was in County Antrim, in the neighborhood of Ballynure, between Belfast and Ballymena. Have not looked up the source of this information just now. They finally settled in Augusta Co., Va., and the sons, Samuel Doak, Jr., and Alexander Mathes, went together to Washington Co., Tenn., and were on the way at the time of the surrender of Cornwallis. They walked through the wilderness, and Theodore Roosevelt in "The Winning of the West" says that Samuel Doak "drove before him an old flea-bitten grey horse loaded with a sackful of books; crossed the Alleghenies and came down along blazed trails to the Holston settlements." Alexander Mathes gave fifty acres of land for the site of Washington College. He was one of the original elders in Salem church and also a charter member of the college board. There was a memorial window placed in Salem church to the three Alexander Mathes names, who were ruling elders covering a period of 102 years consecutively.

Last year Mrs. Mary Doak Wilkinson, of Telford, Tenn., wrote me about a road that was being improved, which is the old road to Jonesboro, the oldest town in the state, and they had decided to name it the "Samuel Doak Trail," as tradition has it that this was his route when he came from Virginia. That might be an interesting item for your book.

       Sincerely,
         (MISS) I. C. VANDEVENTER.

INDEX

A

Alexander, Rev. Archibald, 38; Frank, 57; Prof. Fred, 57; Jane H., 18-38; Jennie, 16; Mary, 16; Thomas, 56.

Allen, Annie, 19; George J., 19; Wm. Montgomery, 19.

Amack, Thelma, 31; Ivan, 31.

Anderson, Alfred Ewin, 42; Alexander, 55; Alexander Eckel, 55; Charles, 55; Dora, 55; Fain, 55; Frank O., 42; Herbert Gouchenour, 54; Jean Olive, 54; James, 16; Julia Emma, 55; Julia Blanche, 54; Josephine Houston, 55; John Fain, 19; John, 55; Joseph Smith, 55; Leslie, 55; Mary Louise, 54; Mary Jane, 54; Margaret Elizabeth, 54; Margaret Josephine, 42; Rachel Ellen, 19; Robert Doak, 54; Samuel Doak Newman, 55; Samuel Wilson, 55; Sarah Lourinda, 55; Samuel, 19; Susie Ewin, 42; Dr. William Samuel, 54; Helen, 57.

Armstrong, Grace Anna, 51.

Armitage, Harriet, 50; Irene, 50; James, 50; Mrs. James A, 50.

B

Bailey, Mr., 44.

Baldridge, ———, 18.

Banton, Fannie, 54.

Barber, George McKinley, 32; George Higley, 32; John Philip, 32; Margaret Louise, 32; Margaret Logan, 32.

Bates, Ollie, 57.

Batey, Mary, 14.

Bell, Gordan, 22; John Ernest, 31; John Ernest, Jr., 31; John D., 31; Julia Evoline, 32; Warren James, 32.

Bennet, Gertrude, 34.

Benbow, Ruth, 35.

Bovelle, Dr., 39; William W., 39.

Boyd, John, 19.

Billingsley, John, 61; Louise Jane, 61.

Blackburn, Henry Lee, 61; Henry Mitchell, 61; Henry Hatcher, 61; Dr. John Henry, 61 John Denpree, 61; Dr. James William, 60-61; William, 61.

Breckenridge, family sketch, 75 to 77; George, 12; Robert, 10.

Bright, Gardner, 16; James, 16; Gen. John Morgan, 16; Mary, 16; Margaret, 16; Morgan, 16; Sarah, 16.

Brown, William, 13.

Broyles, Adam, 18.

Brooks, Nancy Arwin, 45; Moses, 45.

Bulkley, Charles C., 34; Katherine, 34; Lucy Williams, 34.

C

Campbell, Judge, 13; ———, 4; Nellie, 53; W. A., 55.

Cage, William, 16.

Caldwell, Mrs. J. L., 16.

Carey, Alice, 25; Anna, 25; C. Edward, 24; Charles Henry, 25; Emma, 24; Eva, 25; Edward Montgomery, 25; Frank Niles, 25; Forrest Woodard, 25; Harry, 25; Howard Fenton, 25; John C., 24; Julia, 25; Lucinda Jane, 25; Mary Eliza, 25; Patrick, 20; Robert Lee, 25; Samuel Doak, 25; William K., 25.

Carmack, Hattie McLin, 52.

Cardova, Carlos King, 56; Delfido, 56.
Case, Effie, 46.
Catherwood, Bayard D., 27; Catherine, 27; Dorothy Alice, 27; Josephine, 27; Roger, 27; Judge Samuel Doak, 27; Dr. Thomas Lowry, 27; Virginia, 27; William M., 27.
Clift, Charlotte A. Cooke, 45; Col. Moses H., 45; Nancy Arwin Brooks, 45; Roberta, 45; Col. William, 45.
Colle, Charles Eric, 50; Charles Harrington, 51; Carolyn Louise, 51; Eugene Leland, 51; Grace Anna, 51; Martha Delane, 51; Merrill Doak, 51.
Conn, Eunice Evoline, 33; Frank S., 30-32; Doak Oswin, 33; Julia Mabelle, 32; Lowry Laird, 33; Lucy Elizabeth, 33; Mrs. Lucy Lowry, 33; Malcolm William, 33; Marion, 33; Warren Harris, 33.
Coffey, Alexander Hamilton, 14; Alice, 14.
Cooper, Fenimore, 15.
Courtney, Carrie, 36; Dottie, 36; Lida, 36; Nellie, 36; John, 36.
Cowan, John, 39; Sarah Paxton, 39.
Collier, Alice, 22.
Cox, Joel, 25; Robert, 47.
Creger, Elizabeth, 11.
Crockett, David (Davy), 12.
Crawford, Clara Evoline, 35; Charles Goodrich, 35; David Benbow, 35; Eleanor Adelle, 35; Florence Maybelle, 35; Frances Louise, 36; Frank Stevens, 36; Harris, 30-31-35; Harris Weber, 35; Josephine, 36; Oswin Lowry, 35; Rebekah Irene, 36; Sarah Grace, 36.
Cummings, Dovie, 44.

D

Darr, Jessie, 24.
Davit, ——, 18.
Davis, J. J., 44.
Dayton, Jonathan, 14-15; Amos Cooper, 15.
Dearmin, Esther M. Lowry, 27.
Delk, Dr. D. L., 14.
Dement, Albert, 46; Huda, 46.
Denpree, Martha Amanda, 61.
Denton, Dixie, 43.
De Wolf, Jennie, 27.
Dunn, Jane, 11; James, 11; Martha Long, 11.
Dutton, Elizabeth, 11.
Doak family of Kentucky, 60.
Doak family of Wilson Co., Tenn., 59.
Doak family of Tazewell Co., Va., 78.
Doak records from Chaulkley's abstracts, 79-83.
Doak records from Sumner's Annals, 83-84.
Doak Wills, 85-88.
Doak, Sketch of Rev. Samuel, 63-70.
Doak Emigrants, David, 9-11-12; John, 9-10-13; Julia, 9-12; Nathaniel, 9-10; Robert, 9-10-11; Samuel, 9-10-12-13-15; Thankful, 9–12.
Doak, Alexander Mason Dixon, 47-52-53; Alexander Cowan, 43; Alexander, 60; Alice Florida, 52; Annie F., 44; Rev. Algernon Sidney, 40-42; Rev. Archibald Alexander, 39-41; Archibald Alexander, 40; Andrew Jackson, 59; Bertha Armitage, 50; Banton, 54; Bettie, 59; Charlotte Lee, 53; Charles Smith, 55; Cynthia Anne Houston, 53; Delia Katherine, 42; Edward William, 52; Edward, 54; Edward Wzelle, 43; Elias Lockert, 40; Elinor (of Em-

igrant Samuel), 13; Eliza F. R., 47; Eliza Smith, 39; Elizabeth Thankful (of Emigrant Samuel), 15; Emma Ann, 42; Ervin Foster, 60; Esther Montgomery (of Rev. J. W.), 39; Eudora Elmira, 52; Felix Zollicoffer, 41; Flora Paxton, 42; Frances, 54; Jane Mitchell, 13; Harriet Alpha Armitage, 50; Hanna Eliza, 52; Henry Melville, 39-40-41; Henry Randolph, 53; Dr. Hubert P., 50; Hugh Keffer, 43; Isabel (of Emigrant Samuel), 13; James Hall, 39; James McClure, 52; Jane (of Emigrant Samuel), 13; Jane Rowe (of Rev. Samuel), 18; James Witherspoon, 39; Joan Christine, 53; John (of Emigrant Samuel), 13; John Foster, 59; John Newton, 39-44; John W. K., 47-51; John Whitfield, 18-19-38-44-46; Julia (of Rev. Samuel), 18-19; Julia Margaretta, 47-54; Kate, 48; Lula, 11; Lucinda (of Rev. Samuel), 18; Lourinda Cutter, 47-56; Luther, 52; Mary (of Emigrant Samuel), 14; Mary (Polly) Montgomery (of Rev. Samuel), 18; Mary H., 44; Mary Jane, 47; Mary Lou, 52; Mary Augusta, 52; Mary Katherine, 53; Mary Campbell, 61; Margaret Lacy, 40; Margaret Louise, 41; Martha E., 44; Mattie Emmons, 52; Dr. Matthew Stephenson, 47-55; Margaret Lee, 56; Maude, 50; Maurice Stewart Armitage, 50; Nancy (of Rev. Samuel), 18; Nellie, 54; Randolph, 54; Richard West, 51; Robert (of Emigrant Samuel), 14; Robert Horace, 52; Robert Campbell, 53; Robert, 54; Robert D., 44; Robert Ebenezer, 47-53; Ruby Oatman, 53; Rufus Preston, 59; Rufus Randolph, 59-60; Sarah, 52; Sarah Etta, 48; Sarah Diana, 48; Sarah Ann Eliza, 52; Sarah Virginia, 53; Saba, 40-41; Saba Regina, 42; Rev. Samuel, D.D., 9-10-13-15-16-17-19-38-46-47-51-55-58; Sketch of Rev. Samuel, 63-70; Rev. Samuel Witherspoon, 18-19-46-47-49-53-54-55-56; Col. Samuel Alexander, 14; Dr. Samuel Smith McEwen, 47-51; Prof. Samuel Snapp, 48-49; Prof. Samuel Armitage, 50; Samuel Harvey, 38; Samuel L. (9th Samuel), 50; Samuel Taylor Coleridge, 39; Samuel Gordon, 41; Samuel Houston, 52; Samuel Kitz Miller, 53; Samuel Langford, 60; Shirley, 41; Sidney Smith, 42; Sophia, 39; Susan Virginia, 52; Stanley Alexander, 53; Thomas J., 44; Thankful Caroline, 44; Virginia Paxton, 41; Dr. Wiley Harvey, 38; Rev. Wm. Stephenson, 47-51-54; William Melville, 41; William Edmonson Kennedy, 39-41; William Clay, 48.

E

Ely, Catherine, 27; Robert, 27.
Erickson, Carl, 34; John, 34; Margaret, 34; Robert, 34.
Eyre, Charles, 32; Delma Marguerita, 32; Florence Rebekah, 33; Frances Eloise, 33; John Ellis, 32; Susan Palmer, 32.

F

Fain, Amelia, 18; Col. John, 19.
Fenton, Martha Louise, 25.
Fere, Ethel, 30.
Feemster, Frances, 57.
Finley, John, 12; Polly (Mary), 12; Samuel, 12.
Folger, Floy, 54.
Fox, Miriam, 34.

INDEX

Forbes, Betty Ann, 36; Ian, 36; Ian, Jr., 36; Jean, 36.
French, Mrs. J. Stewart, 60.

G

Gass, Anna Bell, 54.
Galbreath, Seburn, J., 19; Elizabeth, 38.
George, Enuty, 44; Robert, 44; Susan Lacy, 44.
Gidding, Paul, 18.
Gibson, Dr. Matthew, 47.
Good, Ora, 23.
Goodrich, Joseph, 31; Rebekah, 31; Susan Stevens, 31.
Gouchenour, Blanche, 54.
Gracey, Judith Bright, 16.
Gray, Robert, 44; Susie, 41.
Greer, Ida, 61.

H

Hall, Elizabeth Thankful Doak, 15-16; Gov. William, 15-16; Major William, 15.
Halliburton, Mary Pocahontas, 14; William Henry, 14.
Harris, Elizabeth, 14; Julia Miller, 19.
Hanes, Rev. B. E., 10.
Harrison, Colie, 59; Lucinda, 15.
Hanna, Margaret, 60; Maria Jane, 26; Samuel, 26.
Hatch, Robert, 46.
Harrington, Margaret, 51.
Hasley, Alice, 33.
Haskell, Ernest Hadden, 18.
Hatcher, Bess Trousdale, 61.
Henderson, Dr. Paul, 48.
Hess, Lydia P., 30-34.
Heyen, Clara K., 30-31.
Herman, Elsa, 33.
Hill, Abigail, 25; Elgin A., 35.
Hindman, Darwin A., 41.
Hine, Helen, 28-29.

Hooper, Cora, 14; Jonathan, 15; Ruth, 14; Warren Franklin, 14; Warnie, 14-15; William, 14.
Hodge, Rev. Samuel, 39.
Hoagland, Mary, 32.
Holmgrain, Myrtle, 29.
Holmes, Kate Hinman, 34; Lucia, 34; William Elliott, 34.
Horton, George C., 25; Helen Clifford, 25; Mary Louise, 25.
Houston, Esther, 17; John, 17; Margaret Cunningham, 17; Rev. Samuel, 17.
Humphrey, Jay, 52.
Huguenin, Philip, 34; Sarah, 34.

J

Jameson, Ella, 23.
Johnson, Charles Mansfield, 35; Florence Louise, 35.

K

Karstorp, Gustava, 35.
Keeble, Effie, 57.
Keifer, Gen. Joseph Warren, 31; Joseph Warren, Jr., 30-31; Joseph William, 31; Lucy Stout, 31; Margaret Eliza, 32; Oswin, 32.
Kendall, Helen, 32; Lily Bradshaw, 32; Wallace, 32.
Kennedy, Rev. Benjamin David, 38.
Kindle, Louise, 36.
King, Julia Marianna, 49.
Kite, William, 52.
Koontz, Nancy Lee, 33; Philip Grant, 33; Philip M., 33.
Kreger, Anna Kate, 53; Margaret, 55.

L

Lang, Eva Leonard, 32; John, 32; Margaret, 32.
Laughlin, Almira Lowry, 26.

Lawrence, Fred, 53; Lacy L., 53; Maud Willis, 53; Minnie Lee, 53.
Lawall, Mary, 50.
Lawson, Roberta Jane, 45; Wm. Seymour, 45.
Lichens, Gertrude Bailey, 50.
Lockert, Margaret, 40.
Learned, Albert P., 22; Alice Rankin, 23; Alice Preisach, 22; Betty Lucile, 23; Edmond Phillip, 23; Don Rankin, 23; Margaret Louise, 23; Ruth Eleanor, 23; S. Stanley, 22.
Lowry, Adam, 18-19-25-26; Alexander T, 28; Almira, 26; Almira Julia, 26; Alfred, 26; Anne, 34; Charles Doak, 30-34; David P., 26; Eliza Rowe, 20-28; Esther Montgomery, 20-24-27; Eugene, 26; Evoline, 30-33; Jean Gilfillen, 20-37; James Thompson, 26; Julia Doak, 19-20-24-25-26-30-36-37; Julia Rowe, 20; Julia Stevens, 30-31; John Knox, 20; Lucinda, 27-36-37; Lucy Jean, 30-32; Leander Chase, 27; Louise Talman, 34; Mary Merriwether, 20-28; Oswin Wells, 30-31; Oswin William, 34; Oliver Howe, 34; Sarah Goodrich, 30-31-35; Samuel Doak, 26; Rev. Samuel Gardner, 20-25-26; Theophilus, 26-30-31; Walter, 30-31; William Henry, 26; Wm. Ramsey, 20-30-31-33-35-36; Sarah Elizabeth, 27; Timothy Goodrich, 34; Oliver Howe, 34.
Lynum, Andrew, 16.

Mc

McCarty, Lula Doak, 11.
McClure, Eliza, 52.
McConaughy, James, 20.
McEwen, Alexander, 17-47; Margaretta Houston, 17-47; Sarah Houston, 18-47.
McGuffin, Mrs., 14.
McHargue, David S., 48; Robert, 48.
McLafferty, Charles Lowry, 32; Fred S., 32; Fred Warren, 32; Joel Edward, 32; Lucy Grace, 32.
McNish, Harvey, 37; James K., 36; James H., 36; Julia, 36; Ottie, 37; William, 36-37.
McNutt, Frank, James, 52; Mary, 52.

M

Mathes-Mathews records and letter, 89 to 91.
Mathes, Ezekiel, 39; William, 52.
Manning, Evoline, 30.
Marks, Dr., 53; Lawrence, 53; Virginia, 53.
Mavity, N. B., 11.
Meek, Elijah, 21; Lucy Williams, 21; Rebecca, 21.
Milburn, Knapp, 45.
Merriwether, Wm. Thornton, 28.
Merriam, Isaac, 45; Martha, 45.
Mitchell, Addie Doak, 19; David, 10; Elizabeth, 19; Esther Susannah, 19; Jane, 13; Samuel, 18; Samuel Fain, 19; Stella, 19; Thomas, 19; William, 18-19; William Hugh, 19.
Moore, Elizabeth, 21; George, 21; John T., 21; Lou Rankin, 24; Maude, 40; Oreta Elizabeth, 22.
Montgomery, John, 17; Esther Houston, 13-17.
Morgan, Felicia Lowry, 26; Capt. John, 16; Nancy, 16.
Morris, Daniel C., 48; George, 49; James, 48; Kate Sue, 48; Mable Doak, 49; Maria, 48; Mrs. Margaret Logan, 11.
Morrison, Jesse, 52.

INDEX 97

Murray, Elizabeth, 43; W. R., 43.
Miscellaneous records, 75-84.

N

Nenney, Katherine, 38.

O

Orr, Lucy, 30-31.
O'Connelly, Laura, 37.

P

Parker, Donald Edwin, 23; Howard Ashley, 23.
Paxton, Rev. John, 39; Sarah, 39.
Perry, Eva, 19.
Pierce, William, 25.
Ponder, Laura, 51.
Pope, Winifred, 35.
Porter, Donald, 34; Elinor, 34; James, 34; Lowry, 34; Oliver D., 30-33; Samuel Doak, 33; Warren, 34.
Preston, Arwin Clift, 45; Charles Miller, 46; Elizabeth, 46; Howard Payne, 46; Hugh Lawson, 44; John White, 46; Katherine, 44; Mary Mears, 44; Marjory, 46; Mina, 46; Thomas Ross, 44; Thomas Ross, Jr., 45; Virginia, 46; Walter, 44; William B., 44; William Doak, 44.

R

Ramsey, Earl, 23; Frank Oswin, 21; Fred William, 24; George, 23; Gloria, 24; Harriet M., 27; Helen, 24; Helen Barbara, 22; Herbert W., 22; Isabella, 21; Jane Steele, 26; Jean A., 24; Juanita Gertrude, 23; Julia Doke, 21; Julia, 57; Rev. John, 20-35; John Thompson, 21; Lucinda, 21; Lou, 21; Mary Eliza, 21; Mary Jane, 22; Marian, 24; Julia, 57; Louise, 57; Raymond,

57; Roy, 57; Ruth, 57; Prof. Hugh Trent, 57; Samuel Doak, 57; William R., 56; Wilberforce A., 57; Willoughby Francis, 57; Winnifred, 57.
Rankin, Alice Herberta, 22; Alexander T., 30; Amanda, 21; Arthur T., 21; Dr. Andrew Campbell, 21; Rev. Adam Lowry, 20; Rev. Alexander Taylor, 28; Charles Rule, 23; David, 21; Don J., 22; Rev. John, 20-37; Mary Burt, 30; Madonna Alice, 22; Mildred, 24; Queenie F., 30; Rev. Robert H., 20-28; Richard Calvin, 21; Richard, 28; Rev. Samuel Gardner W., 21; Sylvester, 28; Thomas L., 21; Thomas Bond, 30; Talby, 23; Roger, 23; William, 29; William A., 29; William G., 29; William Roger, 23; Capt. William Alexander, 21-24; Zella Marguerita, 23.
Reed, Myrtle, 34.
Rice, Ethelyn, 18; Flora, 18; David, 18; John Holt, 18; William Montgomery, 18.
Riggs, Hulda, 31.
Rucker, Jane, 46.
Rudduck, Florence, 46.
Rule, Ella, 23.
Russell, Claude, 50; Nancy, 18.

S

Salizar, Francisco Garcia Y., 29.
Schroetter, Prof. Samuel T., 49; Samuel T., Jr., 49.
Seagle, Myra Doak, 12.
Siegfield, Charles Leslie, 24; Frank, 24; Frances Louise, 24; Teresa Louise, 24.
Sipple, George, 50; Harriet Ann, 50.
Shaffer, Alexander, 29; Annie, 29; George, 29.

Shaw, Allan Reese, 22; Benjamin, 41; Fanny Haliday, 22; Helen, 42; Henry Sidney, 42; John William, 41; Josephine Fizer, 42; Margaret Doak, 42; Robert Rankin, 22; Thomas Benjamin, 42; Thomas Reese, 22.

Shields, James, 14; Margaret, 14.

Slayden, Lillian Roberts, 42.

Sloan, Bessie, 53; Clyde, 53; Newton, 53; Mary Katherine, 53; Robert Doak, 53.

Smith, Burgus A., 30; Kathleen, 30; Emma Regina, 42; Jacob, 42.

Smithson, Bernice, 41.

Smithpeters, William, 39.

Snibley, Doak, 53; John, 53; Harriet, 53.

Snapp, Eliza Diana, 48.

Stallcup, Edward, 25; Emmet, 25; Lucy, 25; Sallie, 25.

Stephens, Clyde L., 24.

Stephenson, Florence, 18; Sarah B., 24.

Stewart, Dr. J. W., 49.

Stout, Eliza, 31.

Stowe, Harriett Beecher, 35.

Spichard, Louise, 41.

Stone, Mrs. James A., 50.

T

Tabor, Mr., 54.

Templin, Alice, 22; Olin, 22; Lena Van Voorhis, 22.

Thomas, John Taylor, 36; Robert Harris, 36; Ralph Hastings, 36.

Thompson, Almira, 26; James H., 26; Prof. S. H., 26; Lucinda, 55.

Thuss, Bess, 40-41.

Turner, Anice, 41.

Turney, Lowndes, 15; Ex-Gov. Pete, 15.

V

Van Huss, Mary, 48.

W

Washington College, sketch, 71-74.

Walker, Sarah, 39.

Ward, Fordham, 21; Phoebe D., 21.

Weatherly, Abner, 14; Frances, 14; Madison, 14; Nancy, 14.

Wells, Doak, 52; Sue, 52; W. C., 52.

West, Margaret, 51.

Wemirt, Julia, 20.

Wilson, Austin R., 20; Emma L., 41; Dr. Frank, 42; James H., 41; Mary Louise, 29; Miranda Olcott, 29; Hugh, 42; Rebecca, 11; Margaret, 55; William Doak, 42.

Witherspoon, John, 56.

White, Cleo, 52.

Whitney, George Lawrence, 33; Mary Rockwood, 33.